ALAN TURING'S
CRYPTIC CODEBREAKER'S PUZZLE BOOK

Compiled by Dr Gareth Moore

FOREWORD BY
SIR DERMOT TURING

TURING TRUST

SIRIUS

SIRIUS

This edition published in 2023 by Sirius Publishing, a division of
Arcturus Publishing Limited,
26/27 Bickels Yard, 151–153 Bermondsey Street,
London SE1 3HA

ISBN: 978-1-3988-3246-6
AD011147NT

Printed in China

Contents

Foreword

Alan Turing's last published paper was about puzzles. It was written for the popular science magazine *Penguin Science News*, and its theme was to explain to the general reader that while many mathematical problems will be solvable, it is not possible ahead of time to know whether any particular problem will be solvable or not. He illustrates his point using various homely things such as a tangled knot of string, and the sliding-squares puzzle where you have to restore the pattern by moving squares into an empty space. So, and with neat symmetry, Alan Turing's last paper covers the same subject as his first, in which—as well as dealing with provability testing for mathematical theorems—he set out what is now regarded as a blueprint for a programmable computer.

Alan Turing's role in the development of computers in the mid-twentieth century is well known, as is his work at Bletchley Park in disentangling one of the most strategically important puzzles of World War II, the Enigma cipher machine. The Enigma machine used a different cipher for every letter in a message; the only way to decipher a message was to know how the machine had been set up at the start of encryption, and then to follow the mechanical process of the machine. The codebreakers had to find this out, and the answer was not in the back of the book. Although they did not have computers to help them, with Alan Turing's aid, new electrical and electronic devices were invented which sifted out impossible and unlikely combinations and so reduced the puzzle to a manageable size. And the experience with these new machines laid the foundation for the development of electronic digital computers in the post-war years.

Computers are now commonplace, not only in the workplace and on a desk at home, in a smartphone or tablet, but in almost every piece of modern machinery. Teaching people computer skills and coding are now considered obvious elements of the curriculum. Except that this is not so in all parts of the world. Across Africa, access to computers is extremely variable, and in some countries there is little or no opportunity for students to have hands-on experience of a real computer. For example, in 2019, only 3.5 per cent of Malawian households owned a computer.

The Turing Trust, a charity founded by Alan Turing's great-nephew James in 2009, aims to confront these challenges in a practical way which pays homage to Alan Turing's legacy in computer development. The Turing Trust has now installed over 162 computer labs in Malawian classrooms, which is the equivalent of 81% of secondary schools in the Northern Region of Malawi. The Turing Trust provides still-working, used computers to African schools, enabling computer labs to be created in rural areas where students would otherwise be taught about computers with blackboard and chalk. The computers are refurbished and provided with an e-library of resources relevant to the local curriculum, and then sent out to give a new purpose and bring opportunity to underprivileged communities.

Thank you for buying this book and supporting The Turing Trust.

Sir Dermot Turing
January 2023

To find out more, visit *www.turingtrust.co.uk*

Introduction

One of Alan Turing's best-known achievements was his role in cracking war-time codes, which ultimately helped bring peace. In this book the only war you'll be fighting is one against the puzzle setters, but you *will* be tackling an extremely wide range of cryptic puzzles and enigmas—challenges that would no doubt have taxed Turing himself, or at least given him some gentle amusement. Luckily, the puzzle-setters also want to *lose* these particular battles so, while every puzzle will present a challenge, they are all designed to be entirely beatable. Keep up the good fight and you should emerge victorious.

THE PUZZLES

The puzzles in this book are different to those you will find elsewhere. Each puzzle has its own instructions but, instead of being told exactly what to do, a key part of the challenge is to work out what exactly those puzzle instructions *mean*. Often the instructions will ask you something that seems slightly strange, or which is not fully explained. As an example, the first puzzle in the book asks you to find "something that is a letter short of where you began"—but then leaves it up to you to interpret that as best you can.

If you aren't sure how to get started on a puzzle, take a look at its title. Usually the title is designed to give you a hint as to what to do, so it's worth thinking about what it might mean. Unusual spellings or strange syntax are also another clue—how could you interpret them in a way that connects with the puzzle? Occasionally the title also includes an example of whatever the puzzle is asking you to find, although it will never say so explicitly.

If, after thinking about it for a while, you are still unsure what to do, then you could try taking a break. Often your brain carries on thinking unconsciously about a puzzle even while you otherwise move on with your day—and this can work particularly well if you are able to sleep on it. But, if all else fails, then the book comes fully equipped with a hints section.

THE HINTS

Every puzzle has at least one hint—often many more—and these are designed to be read one at a time in order, starting from the top. Each hint gets progressively more helpful, first attempting to point you towards what you should be doing, and then in later hints often making some initial deductions for you too.

The intended way to use the hints is one at a time, so you would take the first hint and then return to the puzzle to see if it has helped—and then only return for a second, and so on, if you still remain steadfastly stuck. Reading them all straight off the bat will usually "spoil" the puzzle, since typically you'll learn too much too quickly.

THE SOLUTIONS

If you've successfully solved a puzzle then usually you'll know you're correct, since it will (at last!) all make sense, but sometimes the puzzles consist of multiple components where it's possible to solve some parts and work out the overall answer without fully solving every individual bit of it. In such a case you will probably want to refer to the solutions.

The solutions don't just give direct answers, but also include full explanations of how each answer is arrived at—and sometimes they explain any hints which were included in the puzzle or its title too. As a result you can also use them on puzzles where you are completely stuck, since you can use the solution to give you precise instructions as to what to do—and then return to the puzzle and solve it as a more traditional puzzle.

THE CHAPTERS

The book is broken into five chapters, each of which gets progressively harder than the previous one. Within each chapter the puzzles are all intended to be at a similar level.

It's best to start with the first chapter until you become familiar with how the book works, but you can then jump around and solve the puzzles in any order you like – you won't be missing out on any required knowledge by not having solved any earlier puzzles.

Good luck – and have fun!

Gareth Moore, August 2020

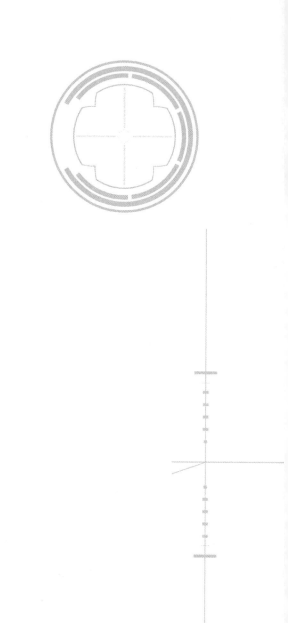

Level 1
Decoded Dilemmas

Alan Turing played a pivotal role in the codebreaking work undertaken at Bletchley Park during World War II. Fellow codebreaker Asa Briggs said, "You needed exceptional talent, you needed genius... Turing's was that genius". The puzzles in this level don't require the same level of genius as they're intended to give you an introduction to the demanding challenges in this book. You'll need your wits about you though in order to successfully crack the enigmas within.

① PATH-OLOGY

Follow the instructions below to reveal something that is a letter short of where you began.

START = Little pigs + Players on a baseball team

MOVE 1 = Quantity of Beatles × Pillars of Islam

MOVE 2 = US drinking age + Digits of a hand + Cards in a standard suit

MOVE 3 = Days in a week + Apostles

MOVE 4 = Harry Potter films + Thieves Ali Baba faced

FINISH = Ugly sisters + Christian commandments

Contiguous US
States

Seventh
Prime

Twilight
Novels

Buchan's
Steps

Numbers on a
Dartboard

Noble
Gases

Horsemen of the
Apocalypse

Musketeers

Days of
Christmas

Adele's
Debut

② ALMOST HOME

What rule has been applied to transform the words or names which form the solutions to the clues in the left-hand column into the corresponding solutions to the right-hand column clues?

Indigenous to a place	➜	Musical set in Argentina
Bring and hand over	➜	Harshly criticize
Dance performances	➜	First name of Blanche DuBois's sister in *A Streetcar Named Desire*
Brightly hued segment of a flower	➜	No longer living
Costing nothing	➜	Indian stringed instrument
First appearance	➜	Cylinder

③ END-TO-END ENCRYPTION

What instruction has been concealed across these three lines, using end-to-end encryption?

Unbeaten natural limoncello; organic craftwork

Vodka adjudicator – reiki impresario – Oahu, US

Cappuccino: occasioned, delicate easefulness

④ LONG NIGHTS

What word might come next in this list?

almond

statuesque

swede

posthumous

unfriend

ersatz

(5) READY, STEADY...

Join each entry in column A with one in column B, according to a consistent rule applied to the things that they clue.

List A

Absent Samuel Beckett character

Trailer; horse-drawn vehicle

Argentinian dance

Transported goods

Large wine jug

List B

Convert to leather

Dessert with a sponge base

Pale of complexion

Round mark

Motor vehicle

(6) SYMBOLISM

If Australia has six, New Zealand has four, Panama and Saint Kitts and Nevis both have two, China has five, and Vietnam has one, how many does the United States of America have?

(7) ACTION!

Can you identify what consistent change has been applied to the following phrases, and therefore restore the original titles?

- ▶ Four Pride
- ▶ Planet of the Shrewdness
- ▶ Reservoir Pack
- ▶ Clowderwoman
- ▶ Shoal Tank
- ▶ The Silence of the Flock

(8) HIGH STATUS

Can you arrange the following clues from highest to lowest?

- ▶ Relating to the body
- ▶ Sports-team leader
- ▶ Bright musical key
- ▶ Not public
- ▶ Widespread

⑨ CHARGED PARTICLES

Join the clues into pairs containing one entry from each column by divining the rule that has been applied. This rule changes each solution to a column A clue into a solution to a column B clue.

Column A	Column B
Very large number	Concerning birth
Placed for military duty	Social equal
Countrywide	Place with a dock
Trailblazer	Writing implements
Retirement income	Bird's beak
Meal serving; segment	Not as much
Female pride member	Clearly expressed

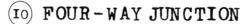

(10) FOUR-WAY JUNCTION

Can you sort these words into four groups of
equal size, depending on their trajectories?

bright

euphoria

cleft

cartwright

countdown

cupboard

frighten

download

group

copyleft

landowner

leftovers

(11) SAY AGAIN?

What property do the following words all have in common?

▶ There
▶ Hear
▶ Fifty
▶ Knock
▶ Now

(12) NEOLOGISMS

Why might the following paragraph have not been able to be fully approved by a prominent authority, prior to January 2020?

"After the unpleasant bridge-burning which had taken place in my old job, I was pleased that the onboarding process in my new job included an informal meeting with the rest of the team. One of the guys, a charming Brightonian, was particularly hench – he must be making good use of the company gym. My boss brought some food for all of us. I tried a macaron for the first time which was wonderful."

(13) MIRROR MIRROR

Which word in each pair is the most reflective?

PAIRED / REPAID

SKINT / KNITS

REVEL / ELVER

REWARD / WARRED

STOPS / POSTS

LEEKS / KEELS

(14) MISSPENT?

What do the following words all have in common?

▶ Clad
▶ Bison
▶ Tallboy
▶ Skid
▶ Canteen
▶ Class

(15) A BRIGHT FUTURE

If its preceding equations are true, what might the final equation equal?

▶ Banana + cornflower = Kermit the frog
▶ Ruby + denim = amethyst
▶ Big bird + blood = pumpkin
▶ Smurf + sunflower = mint
▶ Cherry + lemon = ?

(16) ROLL UP

Rearrange the anagrams below to reveal six types of baked good. Each anagram has had an extra letter added to it, as well as in two cases a space. The extra letters will spell something often associated with bread, when read from top to bottom.

1. GABBLE

2. OUNCES

3. FLOAT

4. NEW ORBIT

5. BE HEROIC

6. CREAK

(17) IN SHORT

The following clues describe the elements of four sets of pairs. Can you put these four pairs back together? The length of each word is indicated.

▶ Liquid measurement unit (4)
▶ It follows midday (9)
▶ Antipodean state (7, 9)
▶ Central American country (6)
▶ Individual's secretary (8, 9)
▶ Precious metal (8)
▶ State with Olympia as its capital (10)
▶ British head of government (5, 8)

(18) SEASONING REQUIRED

What do these clues describe?

- ▶ A message delivered to conscientious farmers after dark
- ▶ Two arrangements of greenery – one is regal
- ▶ Three rulers use astral navigation while carrying valuable cargo
- ▶ A trio of vessels are sighted during a festival
- ▶ A man's footsteps provide respite from inhospitable weather for another

(19) SINGLES BAR

What unites the artists who released the following songs?
The year in which each song was released is given.

- ▶ *She Wolf* (2009)
- ▶ *Only Girl (In the World)* (2010)
- ▶ *Hometown Glory* (2007)
- ▶ *Like a Virgin* (1984)
- ▶ *Believe* (1998)
- ▶ *Fields of Gold* (1993)
- ▶ *Suedehead* (1988)

20 PHRASE BOOK

Six pairs of clues have been split up. Can you reunite them, joining them via the same additional word?

Edible seeds (5)

Underneath (5)

Dry powder (4)

Strip worn around the waist (4)

Jester (4)

Soar (3)

Tip a drink (5)

Frolic (4)

Yank (4)

Avian home (4)

Cut with teeth (4)

Socket counterpart (4)

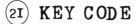

(21) KEY CODE

The names of six mathematicians have been encoded below using
the same substitution cipher. Can you crack the cipher to reveal the
names? The numbers have been assigned using a particular rule.

▸ 10 8 3 4 4 3   13 3   14 3 4 26 11 5
▸ 8 12 11 11 22   25 3 25 9 25
▸ 3 7 22 19 8 13
▸ 19 3 9 25 16 11 4 13   3 7 19 3 4
▸ 12 9 10 16 8 3   15 3 4 26 11 8 25
▸ 10 6 5 16 11 15 9 4 11 12

(22) CHECKMATE

In what way do these real and fictional people form two groups of
four?

▸ Songwriter of *Seven Nation Army*
▸ Character played by Taylor Lautner in *Twilight*
▸ American actor who starred in *School of Rock*
▸ Protagonist of Disney's first animated feature film
▸ Deep-voiced singer of "Can't Get Enough of Your Love, Babe"
▸ English singer and presenter who reached No. 1 in 1964 with the
  single "Anyone Who Had a Heart"
▸ Author of *Charlotte's Web*
▸ Harry Potter's godfather

(23) TWO WAYS

What connects each pair of clues?

▶ Students
▶ Minor mistake

▶ Hand over to the correct person
▶ Harshly criticized

▶ In a state of tension
▶ Sweet treats

▶ Drinking implement
▶ Skin growths

▶ Still breathe
▶ Extremely wicked

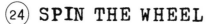

(24) **SPIN THE WHEEL**

Mentally revolve the two inner disks until eight four-letter words are lined up. Each word will begin with the central S and read outwards in a radial line.

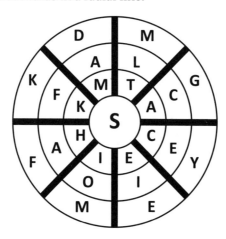

(25) **IN A BIND**

Can you untangle each of these knots?

RLEP

HHTMH

FOEBCE

BIWDIOE

GQAANE

(26) MUCH TO DO

Which Shakespeare play can help reveal the six words found modified and arranged as below?

mew

torn

shw

0

aficion

lescent

reut

(27) LINE UP

A bull follows a ram.

A lion follows a sideways moving crustacean.

A male sheep follows two fish.

Who follows a goat?

(28) ROUND TRIP

Create three new lists by adding a single letter to the start of each of the words below, so that a circular sequence is made by reading the words created by the missing letters.

List 1	List 2	List 3
Error	Alms	Angling
Con	Rises	Spouse
Ailing	Lope	Cute
Bony	Able	Imp
	Quality	

(29) SKIING IS THE OTHER WAY

What word might come next in this sequence?

withheld

bedraggled

graffitied

mouthfeel

swaddled

accountability

cabbages

?

(30) A DANCING DILEMMA

What related word is encoded in the following note found at a ballet audition?

Audition: performance order not finalized

The Rite of Spring, fifth position

Romeo and Juliet, second position

Giselle, fourth position

Rhapsody, fourth position

Three Preludes, first position

The Nutcracker, fourth position

(31) AURIC ADVANTAGE

Which three rules have been used to sort the names in this Venn diagram?

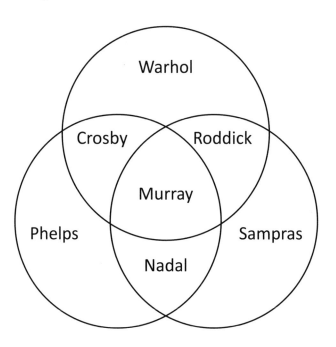

(32) SPECIAL OCCASIONS

Why are the following correct? Can you suggest a word to complete the final equation?

▶ $Wood^2$ = Silver
▶ Gold – Pearl = Porcelain
▶ Wood x Leather = Crystal
▶ Sapphire – Pearl = ?

(33) TANGLED DUOS

Untangle each of the following pairs of related items. The letters in each pair are in the correct order for each item, but the items can be mixed in any way. All spaces have been removed.

SBASKKIEJTUMBPIANLGL

BSIAWTHIMLMINONG

BTORIABSLTHLEIONGH

CUARRCHLEINRGY

JLUUGDEO

SKESHLOOETITONGN

SBANDOWMIBNOATRDON

FIWEGIGUHTRELISFKATTININGG

CRWROESSTSLINCOUGFNTRREEYSKSTIYINGLE

(34) RACKETS

How are the following words connected?

▶ Homework
▶ Embarked
▶ Precooked
▶ Spurring
▶ Microarray
▶ Unmooring

(35) BOARD GAME

Which of these words is the odd one out?

▶ Opportunity
▶ Repertoire
▶ Typewriter
▶ Porter
▶ Pepper
▶ Rotor
▶ Prey

Level 2

Meta Mysteries

Turing's creative thinking led to the "The Imitation Game", also known as the Turing Test. He proposed that should a human tester not be able to tell the difference between the response of a computer or another human, then the machine could be said to be "intelligent". You'll need to exhibit the same abstract and creative thinking that Turing applied as you approach the more difficult puzzles in this second level.

(1) BOUNDARY CROSSINGS

Borders in which country have been crossed in each of the following phrases?

▶ Toga alarm
▶ Sinewy necks
▶ Funny pastime
▶ Pharaoh indigestion
▶ Pilgrims laugh
▶ Kiwi mnemonics
▶ Junior waffler

(2) A SHARP TASTE

Which of the following tunes is good enough to eat?

D F♭ E♯ A B♯ F♭ D

B♯ A C♭ C♭ A G F♭

F♭ E♯ E♯ A B♯ F♭ D

C♭ A G G A G F♭

A B♯ B♯ F♭ D F♭ D

③ STORE THE CROWNS

How can you use "the crowns" to help you fit two stops, two copies, two plays, and two settlements into this grid? Each of the solutions should appear twice, reading once from top to bottom, and once from right to left.

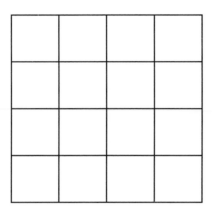

④ MAKE THE CALL

Which country should replace the question mark below?

France + Australia = Sri Lanka

Germany + Russia = Chile

Egypt + Belgium = Mexico

South Africa + New Zealand = India

Norway + Spain = Japan

Austria + USA = ?

5 HANDS ON HEARTS

Something is hidden across these four lines. With which country is it primarily associated?

Indigo dye

Salsa verde

Faint-hearted

Oblique enclave

6 ON TOP OF THINGS

Unscramble the following anagrams and find a word that connects them. Note that although some words have more than one anagram, only one of these will fit the connection.

▶ PIER
▶ AGREE
▶ ONSET
▶ LURES
▶ SOOTH
▶ HEARS

⑦ ESPIONAGE GENERATOR

Each clue in Lists A, B, and C solves to give a one-word word containing exactly three letters. Can you combine, in order, a word from List A, List B, and List C to create each item in the Results column? The lists are not arranged in the same order, and all three-letter words are used exactly once each.

List A	List B	List C	Results
Automobile	Argument	Attempt	Covered in spider silk
Because	Enclosure	Fox's home	Harmonious
Male swan	Male progeny	Place to sleep	Large pea variety
Scam	Network	Plump	Neglected
Spoil	Obtained	Small insect	Walked upon
Wager	Pole	Two fives	Woodwork

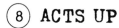

⑧ ACTS UP

Follow the clues chronologically to reveal the initial of a minor character who has the last word.

	1	2	3	4	5
1					
2					
3					
4					
5					

- ▶ "Words without thoughts never to heaven go"
- ▶ "By indirections find directions out"
- ▶ "Alas, poor Yorick. I knew him, Horatio"
- ▶ "Something is rotten in the state of Denmark"
- ▶ "To be or not to be"
- ▶ "This bodes some strange eruption to our state"
- ▶ "Alas, how shall this bloody deed be answer'd?"
- ▶ "The lady doth protest too much"
- ▶ "Frailty, thy name is Woman"
- ▶ "To thine own self be true"

⑨ FICTITIOUS DIFFICULTY

The following book titles have all been manipulated in the same way. Following this system, how would the author of the odd book out in this list read?

▶ YTLBSNSDNSNS
▶ CDJRPDNDRP
▶ MM
▶ KRPDLFSNM
▶ STHGHGNRHTW
▶ NSSRP

⑩ BEST FRIENDS

What connects each of the following?

▶ A US long-distance bus company
▶ A pugilistic, glove-wearing sportsman
▶ Deep and growly, as a voice
▶ An implement used for indicating part of an image
▶ A Scottish water spirit

(II) LOOK AGAIN

How can you add twice, twice to every one of the lines below?

- ▶ Takeover
- ▶ Downtime
- ▶ Lock-up
- ▶ Cross-check
- ▶ Backdate
- ▶ Playroom

(I2) TITLE CONFUSION

The following films and songs have all had their titles changed. Can you work out what has happened, and restore the original titles?

- ▶ A Night in the Life
- ▶ One Fine Morning
- ▶ Die Another Evening
- ▶ A Hard Noon's Night
- ▶ Beautiful Dusk
- ▶ The Sunrise After Tomorrow

(13) EYE LEVEL

Can you establish the rule that has been applied to these words to sort them into the Venn diagram as shown?

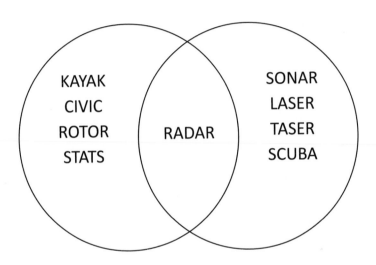

(14) HYDRATION

How could you add the sound of Parisian water to each of the following in order to create something new?

▶ Roll up, as a flag
▶ Became vinegary
▶ CD, for example
▶ Rowing blades
▶ Big puff of wind
▶ Musical group

(15) NICE TO SEE YOU

These clues all describe words with a similar property. What is it?

▶ An overused stereotype
▶ A road with a dead end
▶ An uncanny feeling of familiarity
▶ An afternoon performance
▶ A professional driver
▶ A seductive woman

(16) ORCHESTRAL PUZZLE

Given the following, what might a flute become?

A harp can become either a fish or a long-eared mammal

A tuba can become either a fish or a Caribbean country

A cello can become a friendly greeting or places of imprisonment

A horn can become damaged from use or a painful area of skin

A trumpet can become a flat cake cooked on a griddle

(17) SETT ASIDE

Who's not home?

BIWASPKE	HOOTTERLT
FOHARERM	KENDOGNEL
FORMICARY	SPIGTY
NEOWLST	HIBEEVE
COHENOP	DELIONN

⒅ FIRST FIRSTS

In what way can a "first" be used to create a different "first" in each of these three bullet points?
Can you identify the sources involved?

▶ Creating allegorical literature leaves me exhausted, inventing stories hampers mastery and experimental logic.

▶ In the western area, sometimes animal pastures look endless, almost surpassing Utah's rolling expanses. The oxen become unrecognizably, remorselessly nebulous.

▶ After leaving Laurie, Cathy had impishly leaped down, running ever nearer, expecting Xavier's call. Empty paths twisted over new, earthy ground, running over winding, undulating province.s

⒆ IN ANOTHER TECHNICAL AREA

If Denmark is CPH, Norway is OSL, and Finland is HEL, what is Sweden?

(20) ABSENCES

What has happened here? What does each line of this image represent?

IR MP

ONDON PN

WID ERIC

Y OK

DR

DR

M

ALL ELS LEAVE ELSE LEAVE ALL EVE ALL

(21) YOU'VE GOT MAIL

What do the following have in common?

▶ Tropical American animal similar to an alligator
▶ Bruce Wayne's alter ego
▶ Angela Merkel's native language
▶ A type of low seat that can also serve as a storage space
▶ The 33rd president of the USA

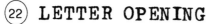

(22) LETTER OPENING

How can the following clues be sorted into two sets of equal size?

▶ A decorative member of the crow family
▶ Expanse of water
▶ For what purpose?
▶ Visual organ
▶ Small green vegetable
▶ Have a need to repay
▶ Hive-dwelling insect
▶ A female sheep

23 COOPED UP

What group of words have escaped together, leaving the spaces below?

_ _ _ CALL

_ _ _ WOOD

_ _ _ TAILS

_ _ _ _ WIFE

_ _ _ LICK

_ _ _ _ _ PLAY

24 ROUND BRITAIN TOUR

The following places are linked by a progressive theme. Which place can be linked in THREE consecutive ways?

ETON

WYTON

CHERTSEY

HURLFORD

FORTEVIOT

AXMINSTER

INVERCASSLEY

HIGHER DINTING

HIDDEN CONNECTIONS

A different group of related things has been hidden in each of these sets of five words. What is the hidden grouping in each set?

Set 1

SCHADENFREUDE

ASPIRANTS

EGOMANIAC

INCUBATION

HESPERUS

Set 2

GUNFIRE

CLOAKED

HELMET

HAPPINESS

FACEPALMING

Set 3

ESCARPMENT

SPIKED

FREELOADER

ENCODING

TUNABLE

Set 4

SUBLIMELY

APPEARING

SEDATED

EFFIGY

GRAPPLER

㉖ REMORSE ON THE RADIO

What coding scheme and device can be used to turn each item in
List A into its counterpart in List B? The lists are arranged in the
same order.

List 1		List 2
Golf	→	Whiskey
Uniform	→	Delta
Lima	→	Foxtrot
Alpha	→	November
Quebec	→	Yankee
Victor	→	Bravo

㉗ KNOW-ALLS

What connects the following clues?

- ▶ Perfect; without blemish
- ▶ Signal giving the go-ahead
- ▶ Organized arrangement
- ▶ Angel's accessory
- ▶ Liberty
- ▶ Impossible to find a substitute for

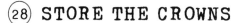

(28) STORE THE CROWNS

How can you use "the crowns" to help you fit two stops, two copies, two plays, and two settlements into this grid? Each of the solutions should appear twice, reading once from top to bottom, and once from right to left.

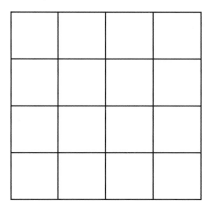

(29) MARRIAGE THERAPY

Can you suggest one of various last names that could come next in this sequence?

▶ Zeta-Jones
▶ Frank
▶ Fonda
▶ Hathaway
▶ Tate

(30) SCIENTIFIC STATES

What number should be assigned to Nebraska in the following list?

Arkansas (18)

California (20)

Colorado (27)

Georgia (31)

Indiana (49)

Minnesota (25)

Nebraska (?)

(31) BUILD YOUR OWN PALINDROME I

Solve the clues below, which have been arranged in alphabetical order of their answers. Then rearrange the answers so that together they form a palindrome.

▶ Famous volcano (4)
▶ Gad about (9)
▶ German wine (7)
▶ Descendant of Noah's son (6)   Occasionally (9)
▶ Form of pasta (11)
▶ Follow too closely, perhaps (8)
▶ Small settlement (7)

(32) SLOOP POOLS

Mentally revolve the two inner disks until eight four-letter words are lined up. Each word will begin with the central S and read outwards in a radial line.

When all the words are correctly lined up, each revealed word should also be reversible, i.e. able to be read, as a new word, from the outside in.

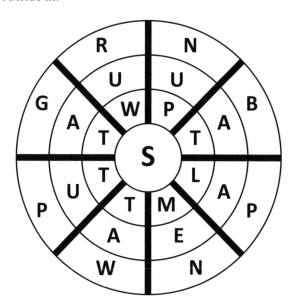

Level 3
Cryptic Conundrums

Turing is considered the "father of modern computing". He displayed great ingenuity in his ideas, such as in his design for the Automatic Computing Engine (ACE) and in giving the first known lecture on "computer intelligence" in 1947. The same ingenuity of thinking Turing displayed will be needed as you tackle the puzzles in this third level of tougher conundrums.

(1) TYPECAST

What question arises from following these instructions?

▶ E → C → T → B → U

▶ R → V → F → H → Y → N

▶ 4 → T → 7 → T → V

(2) JOIN THE - DOTS -

Given that...

A + O = 1

U + M = 2

I + W = 3

H + T = 4

A + T = W

... what code is formed by the following equations?

T + T

T + M

E + N

I + E

I − E

(3) ANIMAL CHARACTERS

Sort the literary animals below into three groups of equal size, based on fictional groupings.

Cat

Mole

Tiger

Caterpillar

Rabbit

Wolf

Hare

Water vole

Black panther

Badger

Bear

Toad

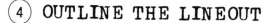

(4) OUTLINE THE LINEOUT

The title of which animated film sums up the state of these words?

sprin	sinh
uncinh	moutd
boutgo	marouta
infox	joutx
adoroutg	sproutg
abin	yinh
moutor	loute
scined	snin

(5) NAME DROPPING

Work out which people are being described, then suggest who might come next in the following sequence:

- ▶ Founder of a well-known distillery in Tennessee
- ▶ British actor known for his role in the *James Bond* franchise
- ▶ British R&B artist who released the album *The Time Is Now* in 2018
- ▶ Prime Minister of the UK from 1916 to 1922
- ▶ Member of The Beatles who wrote *Something*
- ▶ _____ ?

(6) THE ROOT OF THE PROBLEM

These clues all describe words or phrases with a similar property. What is it?

▶ Evidence that someone was not present when a crime took place (5)
▶ Repeated to the point of tiresomeness (2, 7)
▶ Sense of self-importance (3)
▶ Grounds and buildings of a university (6)
▶ Amount added to salary (5)
▶ Former student (7)
▶ The other way around (4, 5)

(7) FAMOUS FIGURES

Can you identify which well-known figures have been disguised below, and what rule has been applied?

▶ Marilyn Madison
▶ Howard Ford
▶ Elizabeth Polk
▶ George Cleveland
▶ Henry Nixon
▶ Samuel Lincoln

⑧ READ THE SIGNALS

Based on the encoded meanings of the departure times, which ship berth is the odd one out?

Ship berth	Departure times						
1	09:20	19:30	19:50	19:10			
2	07:15	19:30	09:20	10:00			
3	09:15	10:10	18:00	18:00	18:10	09:15	
4	09:30	10:45	13:15				
5	07:00	06:10	18:10	19:10			
6	10:30	19:30	09:00	10:00	19:30	19:50	19:20
7	06:00	06:10	10:30	19:00			
8	07:45	10:10	19:10	19:10			

⑨ ALL THAT GLISTERS

Can you reveal the quotations concealed by each of the following lines, which have been encoded in a consistent way, and identify their common source?

▶ NWST HWN TRFR DSC NTNT
▶ LLM TBY MN LGHT PR DTTN
▶ FRS FLN DFL SFR
▶ FRND SRMN SCNT RYM NLN DMY RRS
▶ FMS CBTH FDF LVP LYN
▶ PR FST RCR SSDL VRST KTH RLF

⑩ NOAH'S ARK

What do the following animals have in common?

▶ Black rat
▶ Red fox
▶ Eurasian lynx
▶ American bison
▶ Short-tailed chinchilla
▶ Whooper swan

(II) LEGENDARY CELLS

Can you work out what the rule each circle of this Venn diagram uses to classify the following?

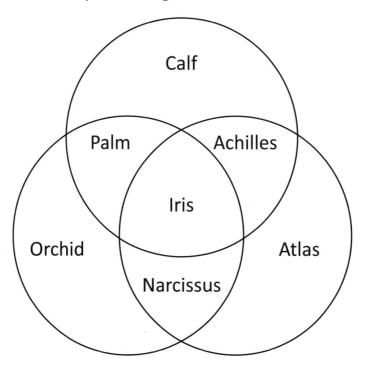

(12) A BIT FISHY

What letter has been poached from within each short group of letters? And what, then, has been poached from each line?

ahe	bw	iea					
eb	gol	ah	ah				
eu	gol	ahe	si	el	ac	el	ise
uper	ise	gol	ar	ahe	el		
aom	ac	bw	bzz	aom			

(13) NUMBER SEARCH

Start as indicated and then key in the instructions below. What number do you end up with?

▶ **Start**: a tool used for golf

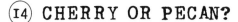

(14) CHERRY OR PECAN?

Can you reveal a quotation from a well-known mathematician which has been concealed within this paragraph using his own constant? What is the quotation, and who is the mathematician?

> I will give you a gift when you arrive. Me, the miserly relation! It will be a gift to intrigue you. Place it wherever you like. Maybe you would like to ask me about its history? It has quite a past: If you can stand to listen, I will tell you about its extraordinary journey. Intrigue and scandal have followed it around the world. There are many tales, but I know only a small part of its journey. People believe what they will, and fill in the blanks with their own inventions. I shall move all other commitments to tell you what I know. As you learn about the manner in which I came to acquire it, please reserve your judgement. There are indeed many mysterious things on this earth.

(15) THE MOVABLE EQUATION

The equation below is a trivial one, but can you move two *different* digits and nothing else, in such a way as to make the equation a more powerful one?

$$2592 = 2592$$

(16) CINEMATIC EFFECT

Can you rearrange each of the letter strings below, then organize these items into three categories?

Each category has a different number of items in it.

TROJ

POTOT

PATO

CATO

KOTRT

SORT

AFT

TTT

STOR

HAN

OSCT

BEST

FOGT

PHBT

TOTR

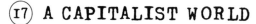

(17) A CAPITALIST WORLD

What do these countries have in common?

- ▶ Kuwait
- ▶ Singapore
- ▶ Mexico
- ▶ Panama
- ▶ Guatemala

(18) SUSTAINED STRUCTURE

Can you crack the number code and work out what is being held captive in the middle of this diamond?

7 2 3

3 2 7 4

3 6 2 7 4

7 2 6 3 5 4

7 2 1 3 5 6 4

7 6 8 3 2 1 5 4

7 8 6 1 9 2 3 5 4

2 7 6 8 1 3 5 4

7 6 2 8 4 5 1

7 5 2 6 1 4

7 5 2 1 4

7 2 1 5

7 2 1

(19) FAMOUS LINES

What connects the following quotations from well-known films, plays, and musicals?

▶ "Baby, Zed's dead" (*Pulp Fiction*)
▶ "My kingdom for a horse!" (*Richard III*)
▶ "Hey, Stella" (*A Streetcar Named Desire*)
▶ "Glorious food" (*Oliver!*)
▶ "And then, put out the light" (*Othello*)

(20) LIGHT, LONG, OR FULL?

The following clues describe phrases that have something in common. Can you identify the common factor and organize them into three pairs based on the factors they share? The length of each word in each answer is given.

▶ At a disadvantage (2, 3, 4, 4)
▶ Cowboy's headgear (3-6, 3)
▶ Definitely not drunk (5-4, 5)
▶ Make a special effort (2, 3, 5, 4)
▶ Shylock's demand (5, 2, 5)
▶ Tiny (4-5)

(21) BASIC COMPOSITION

How can the following compounds be sorted into two groups of equal size, based on their composition?

4 + 18

27 + 39 + 8 + 52

53 + 75 + 57 + 60

42 + 11 + 27

42 + 92 + 34

10 + 15 + 13

88 + 6 + 27 + 8 + 7

14 + 7 + 31 + 84 + 75

(22) STATE MATHEMATICS

In what way can the following equations be seen to make sense?

▶ The Sooner State – eucalyptus-loving marsupial = unit of resistance

▶ The Green Mountain State – a French impressionist = a two-letter abbreviation for a 3D simulation

▶ The First State – British singer of "Hello" = major conflict

23 CIRCLE RANGE

Can you establish the rule that has been applied to these words to sort them into the Venn diagram as shown?

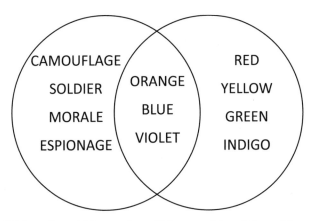

Additionally, which word could be considered the odd one out in the overlap?

24 ELEMENTAL PROBLEM

Fire, water, and earth can all be functioning. But air can not.

Why?

(25) ECHO?

Your ranking in the National Audio Transmission Observatory has been sent to you, but in code. Can you crack the code to find out whether you are on the podium? You may need to shift your perspective.

NUHAI

PWBMT

RWMRJ

JGEWG

HIPXE

(26) QUITE CONTRARY

What do the following words all have in common?

▶ Clip
▶ Lease
▶ Weather
▶ Sanction
▶ Left
▶ Dust

(27) INTERESTING CHARACTERS

Can you restore the confused novels and their authors?

- ▶ *Agnes Jones* by Leo Fielding
- ▶ *Anna Twist* by Anne Eliot
- ▶ *Robinson Marner* by Henry Brontë
- ▶ *Mary Grey* by Daniel Blackmore
- ▶ *Jane Crusoe* by Charles Travers
- ▶ *Oliver Doone* by P.L. Defoe
- ▶ *Silas Karenina* by R.D. Brontë
- ▶ *Tom Eyre* by George Tolstoy
- ▶ *Lorna Poppins* by Charlotte Dickens

(28) ACROSS THE DEEP BLUE SEA

Which of these sea journeys is the odd one out?

- ▶ Odessa, Ukraine to Istanbul, Turkey
- ▶ Qingdao, China to Incheon, South Korea
- ▶ Archangel, Russia to Belomorsk, Russia
- ▶ Bari, Italy to Split, Croatia
- ▶ Jeddah, Saudi Arabia to Massawa, Eritrea

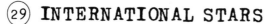

(29) INTERNATIONAL STARS

Can you match each person described below with an appropriate country from the list in the right-hand column?

Songwriter who wrote *White Christmas* and *God Bless America*

UK

Socialite; great-granddaughter of a well-known hotelier

Germany

Pseudonym of the author of *The Call of the Wild*, whose real name was John Griffith Chaney

Italy

Actor who played Legolas in *The Lord of the Rings* film trilogy

France

Screenwriter and director known for *Lost in Translation, Somewhere,* and *Marie Antoinette*

USA

Nurse known as "The Lady with the Lamp"

Bulgaria

(30) AS I WAS SAYING

Can you say what connects the following descriptions?

▶ Undiscussed subject that is looming over a group
▶ Prematurely reveal a secret
▶ A fruitless mission for something impossible to find
▶ A small action that generates a disproportionately bad reaction
▶ Advice to not assume an outcome too hastily

(31) ELEVEN OF TWELVE

Three letters have been removed from each of the following words. In addition to the missing letters shown below, what else is missing?

TUR _ _ _ ER

LI _ _ _ OAT

UP _ _ _ KET

HOU _ _ _ LANT

MAL _ _ _ OPISM

CONC _ _ _ ION

L _ _ _ HTER

DIS _ _ _ ED

_ _ _ GLING

IN _ _ _ CTION

UN _ _ _ IDED

(32) HE-LEXICAL CONUNDRUM

Can you place all of the listed words into the spiral, with one letter per cell? One letter is given. Once complete, a further twisted spiral, of a kind, will be found in the shaded squares.

ACNED	LOSE	PLATE	SEA
CAMEO	MAESTRO	POEM	TERSER
DROP	METAL	PREP	TILES
FOR	MIRES	PROF	UPPER
IMP	OLDEN	PURE	
LIT	ORDER	RETORT	

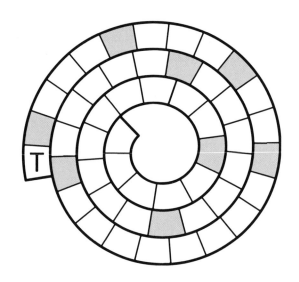

(33) BOUNCE BACK

What do the following words have in common?

▶ Peace
▶ Preserved
▶ Bulletin
▶ Rollover
▶ Unbreakable
▶ Literally

(34) CONTRARY PAIRS

Which of these pairs of words is a "tourist"?

▶ binocular eyesight
▶ spryest anorak
▶ unknown dyes
▶ canonical ratatouille
▶ normal polyester
▶ snore goodbyes

(35) VICTORIOUS

What number and country would be next in the following sequence?

4 = Brazil

8 = Italy

3 = Spain

7 = Germany

? = ???

(36) WORD CONNECTIONS

What etymological feature connects all of the following words?

Cheetah

Dungarees

Chintz

Loot

Dinghy

Jungle

Level 4

Perplexing Puzzles

Turing's colleagues, who were struck by the depth and originality of his intellect, referred to him as "Prof". Put your own intelligence to the test as you attempt to crack the highly perplexing puzzles in this penultimate level.

(I) LONERS

In what way can the following words be considered to have something in common by virtue of having nothing in common?

- ▶ Ambidextrous
- ▶ Demonstrably
- ▶ Lexicography
- ▶ Nightwalkers
- ▶ Incomputable
- ▶ Bankruptcies

(2) SINK OR SWIM

What has happened to all of the boats above the surface, and what has happened to all of the boats below the surface?

CNE   CTMN   CLIPPE   GLLEN   NWBT   SCHNE

- -

NO   MN   LIPP   GLLON   NOWBO   SHOON

(3) COUPLES' RETREAT

Which of the following definitions is the odd one out? The length of each word is given.

- ▶ One employed to keep financial records (10)
- ▶ State capital of Florida (11)
- ▶ Inflatable decoration (7)
- ▶ Major North American river (11)
- ▶ Advisory group, generically (9)
- ▶ Nashville state (9)

(4) BESTSELLERS

What do these clues describe? What connects them?

- ▶ Weekend-evening illness
- ▶ Reports of unknown reliability
- ▶ Flying mammal leaves a satanic place
- ▶ The unlit face of a planet-orbiting body
- ▶ Legal drinking age, in the US

⑤ EASY PIECES

Pair up these words, then order the pairs from smallest to largest.
Which combination creates the odd one out?

baby

card

chest

dates

days

dollar

first

inch

jump

later

street

stud

⑥ ONE STEP AT A TIME

How can you start with a gnaw,

then add R to make a group,

then add T to make it sour,

then add L to make it fragile,

then add O to make a songbook?

⑦ BLACK, NOT WHITE

Fill in the various blanks to make each line musically consistent.

- ▶ _BASEMENT   _____BREAD
- ▶ _LASTING   _____FISH
- ▶ _ENSURE   _____SHOOTER
- ▶ _ALLIANCE   MUD_____
- ▶ _VALUATION   _____LINES
- ▶ _RIGHTFUL   _____-TONGUED
- ▶ _LANCE   _____-EYED

⑧ HIDE AND SEEK

If Scot, Brad, Kat, and Bert are all hiding in Canada, then where are Lori, Diana, Sian, Mary, and Carol hiding?

⑨ CHARACTER REFERENCE

What literary connection do the following people share?

▶ Actor who played Will Turner in the *Pirates of the Caribbean* franchise
▶ Actor who played Samantha in *Sex and the City*
▶ German model and actor; host of *Project Runway*
▶ Early English queen, wife of William the Conqueror
▶ Actor who played Princess Leia in the *Star Wars* films
▶ 18th president of the USA; leader of the Union Army during the American Civil War
▶ Actor who played Vicky in the Woody Allen film *Vicky Cristina Barcelona*

(10) NEAT HANDWRITING

What feature do the following words all have in common?

▶ Numerous
▶ Assume
▶ Occurrences
▶ Merman
▶ Zones
▶ Overarm

(11) LEADING LETTERS

The countries below can be sorted into three lists of four. Which country belongs in each list, and why?

▶ Bosnia and Herzegovina
▶ Brazil
▶ Bulgaria
▶ Germany
▶ Hungary
▶ Oman
▶ Philippines
▶ Russia
▶ South Korea
▶ Spain
▶ Sweden
▶ Thailand

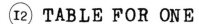 (I2) TABLE FOR ONE

The entries on this menu all have something in common. What is it?

Aperitif

Prosecco with peach puree

Appetizer

Oysters cooked with butter, herbs, and breadcrumbs

Main Course

Beef cooked in a sour cream sauce

Dessert

Meringue filled with whipped cream and fruit

Peaches with ice cream and raspberry sauce

(13) UNDERCOVER

Which of the following is the odd one out?

- ▶ H by J B
- ▶ H by J C
- ▶ A A T W by J H E
- ▶ I A B by S M
- ▶ B Y T by J M
- ▶ R by A F
- ▶ I W A L Y by W H

(14) POETRY CORNER

What property is shared by these notable names?

Charles Dickens

Edmund Spenser

Geoffrey Chaucer

Laurence Olivier

Rudyard Kipling

Thomas Hardy

(15) CORRESPONDENCE

Can you find the missing links between these word pairs to work out which of the options from 1 to 6 is the most appropriate overall solution?

SOME ___ NOT

OVERS ___ VASES

DRAB ___ OWED

OUT ___ TEST

BREAK ___ FLOW

SIGN ___ CARD

CHATTER ___ BOARD

Possible Solutions:

1. Pineapple

2. Panda

3. Envelope

4. Superman

5. Sports

6. Oak

(16) HEBDOMADAL PROBLEM

What is the common factor between all eight of these song lyrics?
Given this factor, can you join them into pairs?

▶ 7 am, waking up in the morning
  Gotta be fresh, gotta go downstairs

▶ She would never say where she came from
  Yesterday don't matter if it's gone

▶ It's getting late have you seen my mates
  Ma tell me when the boys get here

▶ I know a girl from a lonely street
  Cold as ice cream but still as sweet

▶ There's a stranger in my bed
  There's a pounding in my head

▶ Trudging slowly over wet sand
  Back to the bench where your clothes were stolen

▶ Train roll on, on down the line
  Won't you please take me far away?

▶ Hey, man I'm alive
  I'm takin' each day and night at a time

(17) ALPHABET SUMS

In the following equations, each letter stands for a different digit between 0 and 9. Can you solve them both? The values of the letters may change or remain the same between the two equations.

a) ALAN + TURING = GERMAN − ENIGMA

b) ALAN + TURING = ENIGMA − GERMAN

(18) NOT TO BE?

What do the following have in common?

▶ Musical composed by Leonard Bernstein, first performed in 1957

▶ 2006 American romantic comedy, starring Amanda Bynes and Channing Tatum

▶ 1999 American romantic comedy, starring Julia Stiles and Heath Ledger

▶ 1994 Disney animation, starring Matthew Broderick, Rowan Atkinson, and Whoopi Goldberg

▶ 1985 film directed by Akira Kurosawa, whose main character is a Sengoku warlord

▶ Musical composed by Cole Porter, which won the Tony Award for Best Musical in 1949

(19) GNEISS TRY

Solve the clues, then pair each item in List A with an item in List B, according to what's "here."

List A	List B
collier rope	data unit
deadly gnash	hebdomadal lodger
feebly boundary	maritime party
humbugs encounter	ocean atmosphere
spot inheritor	pulverize flesh
umbilicus cry	sad notes

(20) CLIMBING

Can you place these words into ascending order?

▶ Decimate
▶ Triassic
▶ Unity
▶ Fortnight
▶ Quarantine
▶ Score

㉑ CHEMYSTERY

If I expand this chemical compound, and then restructure it, is it harmful or not?

$$CIN_2O_2SU_2$$

㉒ 'TIS THE SEASON

What links the words in column A, and what links the words in column B? And what links those two links?

Column A	Column B
Card	Smoke
Dust	Key
Plate	Tree
Thread	Fairy
Rush	Onion

(23) DREAM BIG

Three pairs have been mixed up below. Can you find a connection to put the pairs back together, and in the process reveal a seventh person who is hiding?

- ▶ Lead singer of Coldplay
- ▶ Leading figure of the Reformation
- ▶ Author of *The Shining*
- ▶ Comic partner of Jerry Lewis
- ▶ American singer who released *Tapestry* in 1971
- ▶ The eponymous character of British TV series starring Idris Elba

(24) LAST WORD

Which four-word film title can be deduced from the following?

- ▶ Awe, tire, two, whole
- ▶ A, god, lady, child
- ▶ Cub, pulp, perm, orb
- ▶ Ears, snaps, ups, pots

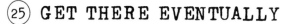

(25) GET THERE EVENTUALLY

The solutions to these clues all have one particle in common. What is it? Once you have solved the clues and uncovered the particle, combine it with a conjunction to form a similar, but inverted, solution.

▶ Giving details of events in the order they happened
▶ Moving in the same direction, close together
▶ Manner in which animals entered the ark
▶ A way to guide someone through stages of a task
▶ Done gradually, a small amount at a time

(26) KEY PATH

What do all of the following words have in common?

▶ Dessert
▶ Sawed
▶ Assessed
▶ Weeds
▶ Lollop
▶ Redress

(27) PLENTY OF MOVEMENT

What connects the following clues?

▶ Provide in small amounts
▶ Sequential diagram
▶ Broadcast online in real time
▶ An event where multiple celestial objects seem to radiate from a particular point in the sky
▶ Arena illumination device
▶ Theory that the poor benefit from the rich becoming richer
▶ Beauty treatment to achieve browner skin

(28) CAUGHT OUT

What do the following clues have in common?

▶ Hot beverage
▶ Robin Goodfellow
▶ Nocturnal animal
▶ Cry noisily
▶ Society dedicated to a certain activity
▶ Actor's signal

(29) A DEARTH OF EVADERS

Can you drop a fifth to crack the numeric code and reveal a villain hiding in the shadows?

6	3	4	2
3	4	2	5
4	2	1	4
2	5	4	2

(30) NATURAL WORLD

What do solutions to the following clues all have in common?

▶ Trendsetter
▶ Siddhartha Gautama's title
▶ Cigar cut at both ends
▶ Giver of obsessive, unwanted attention
▶ Printed flyer

(31) PRIME EXCEPTION

Given the following, what should replace the question mark in the final entry?

▶ BILE = 21
▶ FRANCE = 39
▶ QUENCHED = 47
▶ WEBS = 0
▶ AWAKE = 2
▶ GEMS = 0
▶ COFFEE = ?

③② NO ROOM FOR A TOXIC MIMIC

Can you assign these words to two separate groups, according to their shared qualities? The lists should be of equal size, with one word placed into both groups.

AUTOMATA

BEDECKED

BOXED

CODEBOOK

DICED

DIOXIDE

EXCEEDED

HOAX

MAMMOTH

MAXIMUM

OX

VOMIT

WITHOUT

(33) METHOD IN THE METHOD

What approximate value can be constructed from the series of unknown elements marked "?" when the following transformations are completed?

For bonus points, what additional feature connects the lines, and provides a natural ordering?

Most temperate + ?	➔	Noteworthy
Chart + ?	➔	Fixed
Having the ability + ?	➔	Chart
Fixed + ?	➔	Inhuman
Inhuman + ?	➔	Most temperate
Abridged pound + ?	➔	Experimental room
Noteworthy + ?	➔	Schedules
Experimental room + ?	➔	Having the ability

(34) BORN IN THE USA

What do the following US locations all have in common?

▶ Thousand Palms
▶ Port Susan
▶ Wakarusa
▶ Housatonic River
▶ Jerusalem
▶ Tusayan

(35) LAY THE TABLE

What rule has been applied to manipulate these words, which are given in a specific order?

▶ SAHRE
▶ SCDUHELED
▶ ABOSHELIRS
▶ EMLLISBEHER
▶ OLIGATBE

36 CORRESPONDENCE

Can you find the missing links between these word pairs to work out which of the options from 1 to 6 is the most appropriate overall solution?

SOME ___ NOT

OVERS ___ VASES

DRAB ___ OWED

OUT ___ TEST

BREAK ___ FLOW

SIGN ___ CARD

CHATTER ___ BOARD

Possible Solutions:

1. Pineapple
2. Panda
3. Envelope
4. Superman
5. Sports
6. Oak

37 INTELLECTUAL PROPERTY

How can the following list be said to unite two prominent British locations?

▶ Feast marking the commemoration of the Eucharist
▶ Port in southwest Wales which gives its name to the county it is located in
▶ Central figure to Christianity
▶ Last name of a Scottish businessman who ran Great Universal Stores and set up a charitable foundation which still carries his name
▶ Belonging to a martyr who is associated with a wheel
▶ Group of three

(38) WHAT DID YOU SAY?

What do the solutions to the following clues all have in common?

▶ Shellfish dish
▶ Money given to the poor
▶ One of a pair of oars
▶ Rotating blade
▶ Long-eared animal resembling a rabbit
▶ Detritus

(39) BUILD YOUR OWN PALINDROME 2

Solve the clues below, which have been arranged in alphabetical order of their answers. Then rearrange the answers so that together they form a palindrome.

▶ Ester (7)
▶ Form of dance (6)
▶ Stomachs (7)
▶ Large country (6)
▶ *Great Expectations* character (7)
▶ Injury (6)
▶ French port (9)
▶ Silent (9)
▶ Starter (6)
▶ Gang (5)
▶ Ninth month of the Islamic calendar (7)
▶ Calm (6)

Level 5
Enciphered Enigmas

Turing's genius sometimes exhibited itself in unusual ways, for instance he was known to wear his gas mask while cycling as a remedy for the symptoms of hay fever, an alarming sight for those not in the know! You'll need to engage the same creative approach to problem solving as you attempt to crack the most challenging puzzles yet in this final level.

(I) STANDBY

When each of these words is fully restored, which are in a position to work?

cee	prered
dethre	reends
gdola	sced
iric	tal
madna	tee
miker	unicial

(2) THE AZ OF THE US

What must be voided, for these equations to work? Where does the final equation take you?

Hawaii	+	**V**	=	Delaware
Alabama	+	**O**	=	Pennsylvania
Delaware	+	**I**	=	Minnesota
Delaware	+	**D**	=	Hawaii
Hawaii	+	**E**	=	Minnesota
Iowa	+	**D**	=	?

③ SMILE AND WAVE

How can the following be joined into seven pairs, based on the direction they are viewed from? Each pair includes one entry from each column.

Column A	Column B
AXUM	CAW
BCC	EXAM
CIGS	FEE
EGO	GINS
MENS	SCUM
MOGS	SWAM
NUNS	UNUM

④ SQUARE ROUTES®

Place one letter in each cell so that each word below can be spelled out by moving from cell to cell without using diagonal moves. You can use a cell more than once in a word, including backtracking into a cell you've just used. Every word starts in a shaded cell, and all vowels are indicated by asterisks.

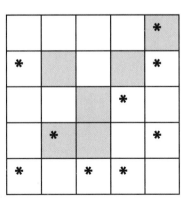

MATHS GENIUS TURING OUTSMARTS GERMAN ENIGMA MACHINE

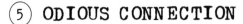

⑤ ODIOUS CONNECTION

Which well-known poet links the following?

▶ Concur (5), avoid (4), gain money (4)
▶ Hotel (3), child's human-like toy (4), tree-like beings in *Lord of the Rings* (4)
▶ Sweet fruit (5), sheepdog (6)
▶ First letter (1), heroic champion (6), metal container (3), strong wind (4)
▶ Expressive exhalation (4), lock-operating device (3)

⑥ ODD ONE OUT

The eleven words below all have something in common. With a little deduction you can divide them into five pairs, with one word left over. Which one?

AMICABLE	EGOTIST
ACRID	FACTUAL
BRASH	ROTUND
BURST	SELECT
CLEANSER	SUPERB
CRUDE	

⑦ ANCIENT EQUATIONS

What are you left with if you:

a. take 2 from either side of 7?

b. take 1 from either side of 5?

c. take 2 from either side of 60?

d. take 3 from either side of 100?

⑧ A SILVER SPOON

Solve these clues in order to work out the rule represented by the arrows:

▶ Lack of polite habits → lunatic pennants
▶ Clears an hour, for example → steals wordless performance
▶ Liking for sugar → chirp old-fashioned truth
▶ Where a car passenger might sit →bag rhythm

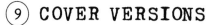

⑨ COVER VERSIONS

A new compilation album features ten songs by well-known artists that have been "covered" by eleven different pop and rock groups. Can you match the songs to the groups, and deduce which two groups have collaborated in one case?

1) Believe
2) Girl From Mars
3) How Long
4) Losing My Religion
5) Mamma Mia
6) Mr Blue Sky
7) Rock 'N' Roll Children
8) Smooth Operator
9) Someone Like You
10) These Dreams

a) BLACK SABBATH
b) KULA SHAKER
c) LEVEL 42
d) RACEY
e) RADIOHEAD
f) SLADE
g) THE ART OF NOISE
h) THE BELOVED
i) THE PASADENAS
j) THE SEARCHERS
k) THE SUPREMES

⑩ A NOVEL APPROACH

This list of works of literature has been abbreviated so that only the initial letters of the title and author are visible. Can you sort this list into three pairs, with one left over? Which work does not have a partner?

D Q by M D C

L M by V H

L I T T O C by G G M

W A P by L T

M B by G F

A P O T A A A Y M by J J

C A P by F D

⑪ ANOTHER GIRL

Which girl is the odd one out on this musical casting list?

▶ Eleanor
▶ Julia
▶ Sally
▶ Charlotte
▶ Rita
▶ Prudence
▶ Martha
▶ Sadie

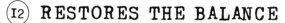

(12) RESTORES THE BALANCE

All of the words clued by List C can be created by combining an item from List A and an item from List B. All of the items in one of the lists, however, must each be used exactly twice in order to complete each item in List C. What are these resulting items, and which list, A or B, must be duplicated?

List A	List B	List C
DUN	DINER	Pertaining to annals
GIN	MICE	Allure
LAC	PORE	Consuming
SET	REF	Method of Braille printing
TEN	SALLE	Fits together neatly
TIN	SET	Provide insufficient finances

(13) VERY THOUGHTFUL

What connects the following groupings?

▸ Scottish church (4), embryo container (3), watch over (5)
▸ Foot covering (4), rodent (3), effortlessness (4)
▸ Length of time (3), horse-drawn vehicle (4)
▸ Top grade (1), joint (5), small child (3), every one of (3)
▸ Take part in a game (4), foot digit (3)

(14) MULTITASKER

Each word on the left, except one, can be paired with exactly one word on the right in a logical and consistent way. The one exceptional word on the left can legitimately be linked to *three* words on the right. Can you match the nine pairs and then identify the multitasker?

BALCONETS	CASTERS
BRANDRETH	CREDITOR
GRISTLE	EMOTICONS
LIGATURE	ENUMERATION
MORALLY	MARINA
PHRASED	PALIMONY
TARDINESS	RESIGNED
TARNATION	STRAIT
TENPINS	UNNATURAL
TRILOBE	

(15) CONTROL PANEL

How can the words PHOTO, BOARD, HAIR, LENT, and BLUE be arranged in the spaces below to make five new words?

_____ + X = ?

V + _____ = ?

_____ + P = ?

_____ + C = ?

Y + _____ = ?

(16) MONORAIL OFFENCE

How many rails would you need to access all of these major train stations?

GDRAEUODRN

AENTLNWRECNRATPEA

LRLEIEPOSREVOTT

GDTRNCNRLAEA

PSIENTTONAN

PIOADNTNDG

(17) CULTURAL OMISSIONS

Can you organize the following into three lists of equal length, based on what has been removed? Each list will therefore have four entries.

- ▶ JA YR
- ▶ ROE
- ▶ CMN
- ▶ OPNY
- ▶ GLICCI
- ▶ HRPRY
- ▶ GUIR'S TRAS
- ▶ TSC
- ▶ HGO
- ▶ ITT WM
- ▶ DID ND NS
- ▶ MMA

(18) FIGURE IT OUT

Can you work out the connection between these abbreviated titles?

▶ A T W I E D by J V
▶ O F O T C N by K K
▶ O H Y O S by G G M
▶ S-F by K V
▶ T T L U T S by J V

(19) FUSION CORE

Can you rearrange these lists while preserving six rows of three items, such that each row reveals a third country, in addition to the two it will already have, when read from left to right?

List 1	List 2	List 3
Angola	Oxygen	Algeria
Cyprus	Phosphorus	India
Guyana	Protactinium	Malawi
Nicaragua	Tellurium	Russia
Ukraine	Uranium	Samoa

⑳ CONNOISSEUR OPERATION

Can you extract one item from each list to create four new thematically linked groups? Each new group must contain exactly one item from each list, and no item is used twice.

List A	List B
GOT	aaiilnt
MAN	aegmnr
NAP	dehissw
VIE	eghilns

List C	List D
Koa	Celsius
Lia	Mach
Pod stlig	Newton
Shillig	Volt

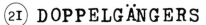

(21) DOPPELGÄNGERS

Can you crack the code to reveal twelve words, then sort these words into three groups of equal size?

1 8 18 5 38 10

2 1 24 30 14

2 30 22 10 16 5 18

3 15 26 9 40 10

7 18 9 24

8 1 32 9 14 5 38

10 5 24 25

11 10 28 5 38

16 9 24 15 23

19 9 24 25

19 21 6 5 38

26 30 11 10 16 5 18

㉒ CREATURE COMFORTS

The following songs, given only as initials, all have something in common, but what is it? The first letters of their common feature spell a word which is applicable to only one entry in the list. The nationality of the band or artist and release date of each song has been given in brackets to help you.

▶ H O L by K B (British, 1986)
▶ A by N M (Trinidadian-American, 2014)
▶ E O T T by S (American, 1982)
▶ K C by C C (British, 1983)
▶ W H by T R S (British, 1971)

㉓ STREPTOCOCCAL INFECTION

Which is the odd song out?

▶ B B by T S
▶ R by K C
▶ T C O T C K by K C
▶ I T M H by W P
▶ S F F by T B
▶ B H by C
▶ B H A T C T by K T

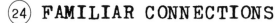

(24) FAMILIAR CONNECTIONS

What do the following people have in common?

▶ Author of *Slaughterhouse-Five*
▶ Actor known for his roles in *A Streetcar Named Desire* (1951), *The Godfather* (1972), and *Apocalypse Now* (1979)
▶ Monarch who instigated the English Reformation
▶ Author of *An Inconvenient Truth* (2006)
▶ Actor who played Sherlock Holmes in Guy Ritchie's 2009 film
▶ Eldest child of the 45th president of the USA

(25) VALUABLE FLOWERS

What rule has been applied to the following flowers? Which number should replace the question mark, and what flower is it then equivalent to as per the rule?

▶ DAFFODIL = 13
▶ HONEYSUCKLE = 18
▶ LILAC = PEONY
▶ ROSE^2 = 36
▶ DAISY^3 = 512
▶ GARDENIA + IRIS = ?

26 CONTINENTAL DISCOVERIES

Eight destinations have been concealed – which is the odd one out?

1. MHBY CEFZ GWKX ODQL UVJTN

2. NFHD IJXLC OVKPW STU QYM

3. GAED HUPJ ZMQR TKVC WXFY

4. AFZJ KLCW OPXQ TVMYS

5. RBFV XJLC QYNW EPTZK

6. MKGO IJZL XQNY WHCF VR

7. HJKS VCLZ FBMX NQTW IYOD

8. YDFU VMHJ KAWC OPSQ XTGZ

 27 RIGGED

What connects each of the following clues?

▶ Ebony hog
▶ Female monarch from Chad's continent
▶ Airborne male from the Netherlands
▶ Walker at daybreak
▶ Four bottles of wine in one

28 VEXILLOLOGICAL VEXATION

What key can you use to decode these flags? Once decoded, which is the odd flag out?

UIBJI CSMD

CJFFY NJOPN

QSFTBNP

QTSNQ SIA QTNBKPQ

TNBMJFJNP

ENJDPI TNBAPIT

OJFAPI SNNJWRPSA

Hints

Every puzzle has at least one
hint, but most puzzles have
several. They are intended to
be read one-by-one in order, so
when you are stuck on a puzzle,
read just the first hint and
see if it helps. If you remain
stuck, then return and read the
second hint, and then so on and
so on for the remainder of the
hints until you — hopefully —
make progress on the puzzle.

(I) PATH-OLOGY

▶ How many little pigs are there?
▶ How many players in a baseball team?
▶ So START = ?
▶ START = 3 + 9 = 12
▶ Every entry can convert to a number
▶ Find the correct answers to the equations, then identify corresponding numbers in the picture
▶ Join the numbers

(2) ALMOST HOME

▶ Once you have solved two corresponding clues, you should be able to spot the connection by looking at their letters
▶ The solution to the first clue in the left-hand column is "native"
▶ What does "almost home" mean?
▶ Return home... almost all of the way
▶ Write the answers to the first column backwards, and you're nearly done

(3) END-TO-END ENCRYPTION

▶ What do you think the title is hinting at?
▶ Have a look at the ends of each word
▶ Both ends, to be precise

(4) LONG NIGHTS

▶ If you have long nights, what else must you have?
▶ Long nights mean short days
▶ Can you see any short days in these words?
▶ "Almond" contains "mon"
▶ Look for abbreviations for days of the week

(5) READY, STEADY...

▶ What do the answers to the clues in column A have in common?
▶ What does "ready, steady..." make you think of?
▶ All of the words in column A contain the same short word
▶ Is this word present in any of the solutions to the clues in column B?
▶ The solution to the first clue in column A is "Godot"
▶ Can you find a connected solution in column B, based on the letters in the solutions?

(6) SYMBOLISM

▶ What does every country use as a visual representation of itself?
▶ You might find this outside embassy buildings
▶ It's a flag
▶ What shape can you find on the flag of each country listed?

(7) ACTION!

▶ Where might you hear the title of the puzzle?
▶ They are all altered film titles
▶ The first title should be "Four Lions"
▶ The collective noun for lions is "pride"

(8) HIGH STATUS

▶ Each solves to a "status"
▶ What connects each of the statuses?
▶ Sort them in order of decreasing rank

(9) CHARGED PARTICLES

▶ What do the answers to the clues in the left-hand column have in common?
▶ What is the general term for a charged particle or molecule?
▶ All of the words in the left-hand column contain the same short word
▶ The solution to the first clue in the left-hand column is "billion"
▶ The solution to the second clue in the left-hand column is "stationed"

(10) FOUR-WAY JUNCTION

▶ What are the possible "trajectories" of each word?
▶ The title suggests there are four "ways" to observe
▶ "Up" is a trajectory
▶ "Left" is hidden in "cleft"

(11) SAY AGAIN?

▶ Do what the title of the puzzle suggests
▶ Try using it as an instruction, rather than as a question

(12) NEOLOGISMS

▶ What prominent authority is concerned with words?
▶ It is a famous reference book
▶ That book is the Oxford English Dictionary
▶ How does this book evolve?

(13) MIRROR MIRROR

▶ How can a word be "reflective"?
▶ The title tells you what to do
▶ These words are not mirror images of one another
▶ Try reading the words backwards
▶ Some of the words are mirror images – of other words

(14) MISSPENT?

▶ How does each word conclude?
▶ The title of the puzzle might help you
▶ What word follows "misspent" in a well-known phrase?

(15) A BRIGHT FUTURE

▶ What visual features do all of the entries in the list have in common?
▶ "Kermit the frog" has something in common with "mint"
▶ "Sunflower" has something in common with "lemon"

(16) ROLL UP

▶ The unused letter in the first anagram is "B"
▶ The second solution is "scone"

(17) IN SHORT

▶ The puzzle title gives you a clue
▶ How might the things described be made "short"?
▶ Look for abbreviations of the solutions

(18) SEASONING REQUIRED

▶ What might provide "seasoning"?
▶ You need to consider the season...
▶ Where might you have heard the events described?
▶ You may have heard them being sung

(19) SINGLES BAR

▶ Why might the word "singles" apply to these performers?
▶ It's not to do with relationship status
▶ What do all of their names have in common?

(20) PHRASE BOOK

▶ The solutions create phrases
▶ "Tip a drink" and "edible seeds" form one pair...
▶ ...clueing "spill" and "beans"
▶ "The" can be added between them to create the phrase "spill the beans"

(21) KEY CODE

- ▶ Each number maps to one letter of the alphabet
- ▶ What might "key code" refer to?
- ▶ Looking at a computer keyboard might help
- ▶ Q = 1
- ▶ And A = 11
- ▶ The numbers correspond to positions on a computer keyboard

(22) CHECKMATE

- ▶ When would you say "checkmate"?
- ▶ What is the strongest visual feature of a chessboard?
- ▶ The answer to the first clue is "Jack White"

(23) TWO WAYS

- ▶ Compare the letters in the solution to each pair
- ▶ View them from every angle

(24) SPIN THE WHEEL

- ▶ Not many four-letter words start with "SC"
- ▶ Can you find a word starting with "SC"?
- ▶ One of the words ends in "AY"

(25) IN A BIND

- ▶ Ten knots are hidden in the list of five items
- ▶ One of the knots is a BOWLINE
- ▶ Two knots are "tangled" to give each item in the list
- ▶ "RLEP" has half the letters of "SLIP"...
- ▶ ...and half the letters of another knot

(26) MUCH TO DO

▶ "0" is nothing

▶ What Shakespeare play has a title that corresponds with the title of the puzzle?

▶ Much...

▶ Add something to each of the six fragments to make six words

(27) LINE UP

▶ The night sky may help you

▶ It might show you a "sign"

▶ A star sign, perhaps

(28) ROUND TRIP

▶ Find new words by adding letters as described

▶ Read the newly added letters together

▶ Read down each list

▶ You should have three words, one per list

▶ These words can be connected by being joined together to make new words

▶ You can connect them in a circular fashion

(29) SKIING IS THE OTHER WAY

▶ All of these words have a shared feature

▶ Are you seeing double?

▶ The shared feature is double letters

▶ Look at the order of the doubled letters

▶ What comes next in that sequence?

(30) A DANCING DILEMMA

▶ "Fifth position" is a ballet term – but what else might it indicate?
▶ Take the fifth letter of "*The Rite of Spring*"
▶ What might "order not finalized" mean?
▶ The letters indicated by the different "position" numbers form an anagram

(31) AURIC ADVANTAGE

▶ These are all last names
▶ Do any of these famous last names have first names in common?
▶ Lots of these people are sportsmen
▶ Everyone except Andy Warhol, in fact
▶ Some of them have struck gold...
▶ ...at the Olympic games

(32) SPECIAL OCCASIONS

▶ What "special occasions" do you think the title of the puzzle refers to?
▶ Each material listed is connected with a certain number
▶ How might an occasion connect with a number?

(33) TANGLED DUOS

▶ Two books from a famous text are included in each pair
▶ The first pair includes Genesis and what else?
▶ And Matthew

③④ RACKETS

▸ What might "rackets" indicate in the title?
▸ Each word is quite noisy...
▸ Look for noises within the words
▸ What do the noises have in common?

③⑤ BOARD GAME

▸ A particular letter is key here
▸ In particular, it makes a word the odd one out
▸ How are the words in the puzzle formed on some sort of "board"?

(I) BOUNDARY CROSSINGS

▶ Where can you find a "boundary" in each of these words?
▶ The "boundary" is the space between the words
▶ What do you notice about the two letters on either side of the space?
▶ How might these letters relate to a real-world boundary?
▶ The real-world boundaries are geographical borders
▶ You will need to look to the "new world"

(2) A SHARP TASTE

▶ Try playing the tunes on a piano
▶ What note is B♯ the same pitch as?
▶ C♭ – "C flat" – means you should play a "B"
▶ For the "flat" notes, you should play one note lower
▶ Do the opposite for the "sharp" notes

(3) STORE THE CROWNS

▶ The given items are clues to words that must be fitted
▶ You are looking for four four-letter words
▶ Pay attention to the title
▶ You must store "the crowns"
▶ Can you make a stop, a copy, a play, and a settlement from "the crowns"?
▶ Use the letters of "the crowns" to solve the clues
▶ A stop is a rest

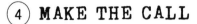

④ MAKE THE CALL

▶ What might "make the call" suggest?

▶ What is individual to a country when making a telephone call?

▶ France = 33. What do Australia and Sri Lanka equal?

⑤ HANDS ON HEARTS

▶ Why might some people place their hand on their heart?

▶ Try looking at the letters around the space or hyphen in each line

▶ You might find what is hidden being performed at the start of a sports match

▶ Take certain letters from the middle of each line

⑥ ON TOP OF THINGS

▶ What is another way of saying that something is "on top" of something else?

▶ How can this be combined with each of the solved anagrams?

⑦ ESPIONAGE GENERATOR

▶ Each "Result" word has nine letters

▶ An automobile is a CAR

▶ Woodwork is carpentry...

▶ ...that is, CAR + PEN + TRY

(8) ACTS UP

- ▶ Where do the quotations come from?
- ▶ They are from the Shakespeare play, *Hamlet*
- ▶ How are plays structured, in terms of how they are divided into parts?
- ▶ Do these sections have numbers that might be useful as coordinates?

(9) FICTITIOUS DIFFICULTY

- ▶ What is missing from the entries listed?
- ▶ There are no vowels – you must restore them
- ▶ They are all well-known novels
- ▶ All of the novels are by the same author, except one

(10) BEST FRIENDS

- ▶ Who is sometimes said to be a "best friend"?
- ▶ This puzzle is animal themed
- ▶ The clues all describe breeds of a certain type of animal

(11) LOOK AGAIN

- ▶ Split each line in half
- ▶ Specifically, split it into two words
- ▶ What can you add to all of these separate words?
- ▶ If you were to look again, you would do a… what?
- ▶ Twice… do it "twice."

(12) TITLE CONFUSION

▶ What can you spot in common between all the incorrect titles?

▶ Do these titles remind you of real film or song titles?

▶ The first should be "A Day in the Life"

(13) EYE LEVEL

▶ Some of these items could be a lot longer

▶ Others of these words are worth reflecting upon

▶ What is the origin of the word SCUBA?

(14) HYDRATION

▶ What word might "the sound of Parisian water" be referring to?

▶ Solve the clues and then try saying them out loud

▶ The answer to the first clue is "furl"

▶ Parisian water is French water

▶ French water is "eau"

▶ "Eau" is pronounced "oh"

(15) NICE TO SEE YOU

▶ "Nice" has multiple meanings

▶ One of its definitions might give you a hint

▶ Are the solutions to these clues borrowed in any way?

(16) ORCHESTRAL PUZZLE

▶ How could you change the word "harp" into a different word, or words?

▶ How might these words relate to the clues listed in the puzzle?

▶ Try swapping one letter in each word for a different letter

(17) SETT ASIDE

▶ What is a sett?

▶ Can you spot any hidden animals in the list?

▶ SPIGTY contains "PIG." What is either side of the word "PIG"?

▶ SPIGTY = PIG in STY

(18) FIRST FIRSTS

▶ What "firsts" can you see in each bullet point?

▶ Is there anything interesting about the first letters of each word?

▶ How might the words that the first letters of each word spell make a "first"?

(19) IN ANOTHER TECHNICAL AREA

▶ This puzzle is a real high-flyer

▶ The three-letter strings are codes

▶ A pilot might be very familiar with these codes

▶ Look up "IATA" codes

(20) ABSENCES

▶ What does the image remind you of?

▶ It looks a bit like a tree, growing above the ground

▶ There are seven trees to find within the image

▶ They have all lost certain features

▶ The features are represented by certain letters

▶ The lost letters have gathered on the bottom line

▶ What could the letters at the bottom spell?

▶ What are "absences"?

(21) YOU'VE GOT MAIL

▶ A homophone of "mail" is helpful

▶ How might this be relevant to the solutions to the clues?

▶ The first solution is "caiman"

(22) LETTER OPENING

▶ What might "letter opening" describe?

▶ How many syllables do each of the solutions have?

▶ Try saying the solutions out loud when you work them out

▶ What do you notice about the first letters of some of the solutions?

(23) COOPED UP

- ▶ Each line is missing a word, which fits in the number of letters shown
- ▶ Add a word to each line to make a new word
- ▶ What might be "cooped up"?
- ▶ What might have the ability to "escape"?
- ▶ When complete, the first word means a disapproving whistle or shout made in public

(24) ROUND BRITAIN TOUR

- ▶ The places all make anagrams of something, with some letters left over
- ▶ The "progressive theme" refers to a well-known sequence

(25) HIDDEN CONNECTIONS

- ▶ Each set of words conceals a different theme
- ▶ Try looking specifically at the letters within each word
- ▶ One of the sets conceals animals
- ▶ Another set has a geographical theme

(26) REMORSE ON THE RADIO

- ▶ The words are NATO code words
- ▶ Each word represents an individual letter, e.g. Golf = "G"
- ▶ Find another code to represent individual letters

▸ You need [to] "Remorse"
▸ Golf = - - - ·
▸ Convert the clued individual letters into Morse code
▸ Do you see anything interesting about List A's Morse, compared to List B's?
▸ You may need to "reflect" on the problem
▸ - - - · (G) is a mirror image of · - - - (W)

㉗ KNOW-ALLS

▸ What does "know-alls" sound like?
▸ It sounds like a last name...
▸ ...of a well-known musical artist
▸ How does this artist connect the clues?

㉘ STORE THE CROWNS

▸ The given items are clues to words that must be fitted
▸ You are looking for four four-letter words
▸ Pay attention to the title
▸ You must store "the crowns"
▸ Can you make a stop, a copy, a play, and a settlement from "the crowns"?
▸ Use the letters of "the crowns" to solve the clues
▸ A stop is a rest

(29) MARRIAGE THERAPY

- ▶ The first entry refers to actress Catherine (Zeta-Jones)
- ▶ The second entry is Anne
- ▶ The third entry is Jane
- ▶ Find a sequence that starts Catherine, Anne, Jane
- ▶ "Marriage" in the puzzle title gives a clue

(30) SCIENTIFIC STATES

- ▶ How might "scientific" relate to the list?
- ▶ Specifically the numbers in the list
- ▶ A particular scientific table may help you…
- ▶ …the periodic table of elements
- ▶ How does this table relate to the states listed?

(31) BUILD YOUR OWN PALINDROME I

- ▶ Once you're confident of a clue solution, reverse the letters of the answer and try to locate the "break" where another answer might end or begin. Use the known letters to match possible answers to the remaining clues
- ▶ The knowledge that the clues are arranged in alphabetical order of their answers is helpful in narrowing down possible answers
- ▶ The fourth and fifth clues lead to the two answers at the beginning and end of the palindrome

(32) SLOOP POOLS

▸ Not many words begin with "SM"

▸ Can you make a word beginning with "SM"...

▸ ...which is also a word when read backwards?

① TYPECAST

▶ What might "typecast" hint at?

▶ "Type"...

▶ Think about how these letters might create ("cast") a path using something relevant to typing

▶ Look at a computer keyboard

② JOIN THE – DOTS –

▶ Look closely at the title

▶ There are dashes around the "dots"

▶ This puzzle uses Morse code

▶ A = · – , and O = – – –

▶ What happens if you join the Morse codes together?

▶ 1 = · – – – –

▶ For the first equation of the code, T + T = M

③ ANIMAL CHARACTERS

▶ Where have these characters appeared together before?

▶ Remember that the animals are "literary"

▶ Four of the characters feature alongside Mowgli in a book by Rudyard Kipling

▶ Four of the characters appear with Alice

④ OUTLINE THE LINEOUT

▶ These words have all had some internal parts replaced
▶ You will need to restore the "in" parts to their rightful places
▶ One of the restored words should be "spring"
▶ Another should be "sprout"
▶ You will need to examine the "in"s and "out"s of this puzzle
▶ "Jinx" has been turned into "joutx"
▶ "In" has been turned into "out"

⑤ NAME DROPPING

▶ Can you spot any patterns in the names of the people listed?
▶ Is anything repeated?
▶ The first person listed is Jack Daniel
▶ The third person listed is Craig David

⑥ THE ROOT OF THE PROBLEM

▶ What is the "root" of each word or phrase?
▶ Are the solutions to these clues borrowed in any way?
▶ What language are they from?

⑦ FAMOUS FIGURES

▶ Can you think of any well-known people with the first names listed?
▶ What has changed with respect to their last names?
▶ Do any of the last names seem connected to one another?
▶ The first person disguised is Marilyn Monroe
▶ What connects Madison to Monroe?
▶ The second figure should be Howard Carter

⑧ READ THE SIGNALS

▶ What sort of "signals" might the title be referencing?

▶ The times are signals – signals that might (once) have been used on ships

▶ Draw the times as hands on a clock

▶ The times represent semaphore signal flag positions

⑨ ALL THAT GLISTERS

▶ What is missing from each line?

▶ A common type of letter is missing from each line

▶ Where does the quotation "all that glisters..." originate?

▶ It can be found in a well-known play

▶ They are all quotations from plays, with certain letters removed

⑩ NOAH'S ARK

▶ What is special about Noah's Ark?

▶ How might you have things two-by-two in relation to these animals?

▶ The common factor is to do with the names of the animals listed

▶ What alternative name does each of the animals have?

▶ Their Latin names

⑪ LEGENDARY CELLS

▶ Who was Narcissus?

▶ Where could you find everything in the top circle?

▶ The bottom-left circle requires botanical knowledge

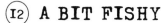

(12) A BIT FISHY

- ▶ One letter has been removed from each short group of letters
- ▶ Restore a letter to each to reveal a set of words
- ▶ What letter has been taken from inside "iea"?
- ▶ "c" has been taken from "ache," for example, in the first line
- ▶ The title is a clue to what's missing overall from each line
- ▶ Work out which letters are missing from each line, and read them line by line

(13) NUMBER SEARCH

- ▶ Where can you "key" things in?
- ▶ What is "a tool used for golf," and what does it sound like?
- ▶ The starting point is a letter "T"
- ▶ Start at the letter "T" on a computer keyboard and then... what?
- ▶ Each line gives you one letter

(14) CHERRY OR PECAN?

- ▶ Think of a famous mathematical constant
- ▶ The title of the puzzle may help you – what can be "cherry" or "pecan"?
- ▶ A pie, which is a homophone of "pi"
- ▶ Count how many sentences are in the paragraph
- ▶ What is pi to this number of digits?
- ▶ How could you use the numbers of pi to choose certain words?
- ▶ The first word of the quote is "give"...
- ▶ ...which is the third word
- ▶ The second word of the quotation is "me," the first word of the second sentence

(15) THE MOVABLE EQUATION

▶ The major hint here is the word "powerful."
▶ What is a "power" in the mathematical sense?
▶ The two digits may not need to move very far!

(16) CINEMATIC EFFECT

▶ How might the letter strings be "cinematic"?
▶ Each of the strings is part of a franchise
▶ You are looking for the episode-specific parts of three film franchises
▶ One of the franchises is Harry Potter
▶ Another is Star Wars
▶ TROJ should be ROTJ...
▶ ...which is Return of the Jedi

(17) A CAPITALIST WORLD

▶ What does the title of the puzzle hint at?
▶ Not so much "capitalist" as "capital"...
▶ ...so what alternative meaning does "capital" have?

(18) SUSTAINED STRUCTURE

▶ None of the numbers repeat in any line
▶ Each line conceals one word
▶ The numbers are standing in for letters
▶ There are animals hiding in the fifth line
▶ The final line is not good
▶ 3 = G
▶ The final line is BAD, in fact

(19) FAMOUS LINES

▶ Try to think of what is said directly before these quotations

▶ You can complete each quotation using only words found in the puzzle

(20) LIGHT, LONG, OR FULL?

▶ The title is a clue to what you are looking for

▶ The first clue describes "on the back foot"

▶ The second clue describes "ten-gallon hat"

▶ What do these two phrases have in common?

▶ They both include imperial measurements

▶ How can imperial measurements be divided into categories?

(21) BASIC COMPOSITION

▶ "Basic Composition." What is another way of saying "basic"?

▶ What are compounds made from?

▶ This puzzle combines several different elements...

▶ ...i.e. chemical elements

▶ The numbers correspond to chemical elements

▶ The first line is "Be+Ar"

▶ Or, rather, "bear"

(22) STATE MATHEMATICS

▶ Try looking at the individual letters of each clue's solution

▶ Look for letters in common within each equation

▶ Try to follow the subtraction operations given

(23) CIRCLE RANGE

- ▶ Both words in the title could be sorted in the left-hand circle
- ▶ Consider the origins of the words
- ▶ Some words have come from a specific other language

(24) ELEMENTAL PROBLEM

- ▶ If something is functioning, then it... what?
- ▶ You are looking for a word which also means "functions"
- ▶ How could this be combined with three of the elements listed?

(25) ECHO?

- ▶ Echo...
- ▶ ...is a code in itself
- ▶ Interesting institution, in the prompt
- ▶ Write it as an acronym
- ▶ The shifts in perspective are Caesar shifts
- ▶ The shifts are not all the same size
- ▶ Consider the positions of letters in the alphabet
- ▶ What do the revealed code words spell?

(26) QUITE CONTRARY

- ▶ How might "contrary" be relevant here?
- ▶ Do any of these words have multiple meanings?
- ▶ How do these meanings relate to one another?

(27) INTERESTING CHARACTERS

- ▶ How have the literary works been "confused"?
- ▶ They have all been mixed up in some way
- ▶ Names have been swapped around

(28) ACROSS THE DEEP BLUE SEA

- ▶ What sea would you have to travel across on each journey?
- ▶ What is shared by all of the seas?
- ▶ The sea you would cross on the first journey is the Black Sea

(29) INTERNATIONAL STARS

- ▶ Can you spot any "international" elements in the names of the people described?
- ▶ How can these international elements be matched with the countries in the right-hand column?

(30) AS I WAS SAYING

- ▶ What might the "saying" in the puzzle title refer to?
- ▶ Each line describes a well-known idiom
- ▶ All of the solutions feature something from the same category

(31) ELEVEN OF TWELVE

- ▶ What eleven of twelve might be present here?
- ▶ From a set of twelve things, eleven are here and one is missing
- ▶ The first word is TURNOVER
- ▶ The second word is LIFEBOAT
- ▶ Look at the three-letter strings that have been added

(32) HE-LEXICAL CONUNDRUM

- ▶ There are more letters than there are cells
- ▶ All of the words can fit into the spiral...
- ▶ ...one way or another
- ▶ The first word, from the given T, is not TERSER
- ▶ So it must be TILES
- ▶ There are 100 letters to place, and 50 cells to place them in
- ▶ TILES, read backwards, is SELIT
- ▶ Which contains LIT
- ▶ The third shaded letter, reading inwards from the outside, is "N"
- ▶ When complete, you should be able to read half of the words from the outside of the spiral reading in...
- ▶ ...and the other half should be read from the inside of the spiral outwards

(33) BOUNCE BACK

- ▶ Do you notice anything hidden within the words?
- ▶ This puzzle has a sporting theme
- ▶ "Bounce" might give you a hint

(34) CONTRARY PAIRS

- ▶ These pairs each have a positive and a negative
- ▶ What positives and negatives are hidden in the pairs?
- ▶ "Binocular" contains "no"
- ▶ All the pairs contain "no," somewhere
- ▶ What is the opposite of "no"?
- ▶ You are looking for hidden "no"s and "yes"es
- ▶ Do all the pairs have a no and yes?
- ▶ What does one pair have instead?

(35) VICTORIOUS

▶ What particular achievement connects all of these countries?

▶ They have all been victorious...

▶ ... in a sporting event

▶ When was each victory achieved?

(36) WORD CONNECTIONS

▶ If you aren't sure, look up the etymologies in a dictionary

▶ What do you spot in common?

(1) LONERS

▶ Do these words have any interesting features, considering their letters?

▶ What letters are in common...

▶ ...within each word?

(2) SINK OR SWIM

▶ All of the boat names are missing some letters

▶ The boats above and below the surface are the same boats, in the same order

▶ NWBT and NOWBO can both be restored to NARROWBOAT

▶ Which letters are missing above the surface?

▶ The missing letters above the surface spell out something you could row with

▶ The boats at the bottom have sunk, leaving no evidence

▶ The missing letters below the surface spell out a way to say "leaving no evidence"

(3) COUPLES' RETREAT

▶ What might "couples" indicate?

▶ There is more than one "couple" (i.e. "couples") in the solution to each clue

▶ Look at the letters in each solution word

▶ Do they all have the same number of "couples"?

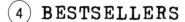
④ BESTSELLERS

- ▶ Why might the title of the puzzle be "Bestsellers"?
- ▶ This puzzle has a musical theme
- ▶ The solutions are all collections of some kind

⑤ EASY PIECES

- ▶ This puzzle is very cinematic
- ▶ "jump" is paired with "street"
- ▶ You are looking for film titles
- ▶ What are all of the pairs consistently missing?
- ▶ "50 First Dates" is a film title
- ▶ All of the films are missing their numbers

⑥ ONE STEP AT A TIME

- ▶ The title tells you how to approach this task
- ▶ What is another word for a "gnaw"?
- ▶ Can you add "R" to that word to make another word for "group"?
- ▶ You will need to move some letters around
- ▶ "Group" = TRIBE
- ▶ TRIBE = "gnaw" with an extra "R"
- ▶ This puzzle involves a word pyramid

⑦ BLACK, NOT WHITE

▶ What letters are missing from the first column?

▶ They are given in order

▶ Whole words are missing from the column on the right

▶ Place words so that each line is the same in some way

▶ Specifically, "black, not white"

▶ Only two different words are needed to fill the gaps on the right

▶ Refer to a piano keyboard

⑧ HIDE AND SEEK

▶ The names are all "hiding" within words of a certain category

▶ How is Canada divided?

▶ What other country is divided in a similar way?

⑨ CHARACTER REFERENCE

▶ What might a "literary" connection mean?

▶ Are there any literary characters which have something in common with the people listed?

▶ Think about the names of books in which these characters feature

⑩ NEAT HANDWRITING

▶ What might the puzzle title mean?

▶ Look at the letters in each word – what do you notice?

▶ Is there something uniform about them?

▶ The letter "y" doesn't appear in any of the words

▶ The letter "d" also does not appear

▶ Why might this be, beyond random chance?

▶ Keep between the lines

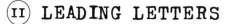

(11) LEADING LETTERS

▶ What might the title of the puzzle suggest?

▶ The leading letter of each country name is a capital letter

▶ What alternative meaning does "capital" have?

▶ What do the capital cities of the countries listed have in common?

(12) TABLE FOR ONE

▶ The appetizer dish is Oysters Rockefeller

▶ The first dessert listed is a pavlova

▶ Where do these dish names come from?

▶ Or rather, *who* do they come from?

(13) UNDERCOVER

▶ This puzzle has a musical theme

▶ The letters are the initials of songs and the artist who performed them

▶ "Cover" is a key word to extract from the title

▶ Can you think of different versions of any of these songs?

(14) POETRY CORNER

▶ What property could these people share?

▶ The reference is to a physical property – i.e. a physical location in the real world

▶ In this case, a resting place

▶ The title clues the name of the resting place

(15) CORRESPONDENCE

▶ Each gap must be filled with an English word
▶ One of the missing words is CAN
▶ Each added word should make two new words
▶ The first line should read SOME WHAT NOT
▶ OVERS + CAN = OVERSCAN, and CAN + VASES = CANVASES
▶ When you have filled the gaps, try reading the added words in order

(16) HEBDOMADAL PROBLEM

▶ A particular group of words is shared by the song titles
▶ Identical words appear in each pair
▶ The title of the puzzle is a clue to this theme
▶ Hebdomadal means "weekly"

(17) ALPHABET SUMS

▶ You can rewrite the equations to make them easier to solve:

$$
\begin{array}{ll}
\quad \text{ALAN} & \quad \text{ALAN} \\
+\ \text{TURING} & +\ \text{TURING} \\
+\ \text{ENIGMA} & +\ \text{GERMAN} \\
\hline
\quad \text{GERMAN} & \quad \text{ENIGMA}
\end{array}
$$

▶ The letters I, N, and T actually stand for the same digits in both sums, so if you can solve one of them, the other one should be easier to solve

(18) NOT TO BE?

▶ Where might you find the words "not to be"?

▶ They feature in a famous play

▶ The plotline of the first musical clued features two lovers who come from conflicting families

(19) GNEISS TRY

▶ Try solving each word of each clue in List A individually

▶ All but one clue gives a two-word answer

▶ A "collier" is a miner; a "rope" is a cord

▶ "Sad notes" – minor chord

▶ Can you "here" any similarities between the solved clues in List A, and the ones in List B?

(20) CLIMBING

▶ What is the etymology of these words?

▶ How might this provide a way of ordering them?

(21) CHEMYSTERY

▶ How can you "expand" this compound?

▶ You need to expand the notation

▶ N_2 can be written "NN"

▶ How can you "restructure" your new letter string?

▶ Are those letters an anagram of anything?

(22) 'TIS THE SEASON

▶ What word can be placed before all of the words in the first column to make five items?
▶ What (different) word can be placed after all of the words in the second column to make five items?
▶ The two words being added (one to the left, one to the right) go together to make a certain item
▶ Counting the words in each column might help you

(23) DREAM BIG

▶ Focus on the last names of the people clued
▶ Do any of them match?
▶ Do you notice another name once you have joined them into pairs?

(24) LAST WORD

▶ What word can you add (i.e. the "last word" of the title) to all the terms in each line?
▶ On the first line, you can add "some" to each word
▶ On the second line, you can add "like" to each word

(25) GET THERE EVENTUALLY

▶ Each of the descriptions refers to a phrase that includes a repeated word
▶ In each case, the repeated word is separated by the same short word
▶ The repeated word in the first description is "blow"

(26) KEY PATH

▸ What might "key path" suggest?

▸ Look at a commonly used object with keys

▸ The words are all of the same "type"...

▸ Try typing the words on a computer

▸ What do you notice about the keys used to type the words?

(27) PLENTY OF MOVEMENT

▸ All the solution words are connected in some way by "movement"

▸ There is something hidden in each answer

▸ Find the connection between the hidden words

▸ The first solution is "drip-feed"

(28) CAUGHT OUT

▸ You might need to read some of the clue solutions out loud

▸ What can be "caught," per the title?

▸ You might find some of the solutions being used on large, grassy areas

(29) A DEARTH OF EVADERS

▸ Each number represents a single letter

▸ Compare columns and rows

▸ 4 = E

▸ The villain is also hiding in the title, to an extent

▸ The bottom row spells AREA

▸ Can you think of any villains with a name similar to "Dearth"?

▸ Their name is also connected to "Evaders"

▸ In both cases, drop the "E"

(30) NATURAL WORLD

- ▸ "Natural world" gives you a clue to what you are looking for
- ▸ The first solution is "tastemaker"
- ▸ Something is hidden within each solution

(31) PRIME EXCEPTION

- ▸ How might you use a letter-to-number cipher code to give values to words?
- ▸ Try adding the numbers in each coded entry together, using the scheme A = 1, B = 2, etc
- ▸ What sort of "exception" has been applied?

(32) NO ROOM FOR A TOXIC MIMIC

- ▸ It's all about the letters
- ▸ Look at the properties of the letters
- ▸ OX belongs in both groups
- ▸ This puzzle wouldn't work with lower-case letters
- ▸ What is special about the letters O and X?

(33) METHOD IN THE METHOD

- ▸ Each line contains two clues, which need to be solved to in each case reveal a word
- ▸ The longest clued word is "timetables"
- ▸ How do you get from the left side to the right side of each line?
- ▸ Are there lots of letters in common?
- ▸ So what do the question marks represent?

(34) BORN IN THE USA

- ▶ The specific text "USA" in the title gives you a clue
- ▶ Do you notice anything repeated in each name?

(35) LAY THE TABLE

- ▶ "Table" in the puzzle title does not refer to a piece of furniture
- ▶ What other well-known table can you think of?
- ▶ How about a scientific table?
- ▶ The title refers to the periodic table of elements
- ▶ What elements can you find in the words?

(36) CORRESPONDENCE

- ▶ Each gap must be filled with an English word
- ▶ One of the missing words is CAN
- ▶ Each added word should make two new words
- ▶ The first line should read SOME WHAT NOT
- ▶ OVERS + CAN = OVERSCAN, and CAN + VASES = CANVASES
- ▶ When you have filled the gaps, try reading the added words in order

(37) INTELLECTUAL PROPERTY

- ▶ Can you think of any "intellectual" British locations?
- ▶ How about places renowned for their universities?

(38) WHAT DID YOU SAY?

- ▶ What might the puzzle title suggest?

▶ Try saying the solutions aloud
▶ Do they sound similar to anything?
▶ The words you need are all homophones

(39) BUILD YOUR OWN PALINDROME 2

▶ The six and eighth clues lead to the two answers at the beginning and end of the palindrome
▶ The first answer is central to the palindrome

(I) STANDBY

▸ There are two different words needed for the restorations
▸ All of the clues need a whole word inserted to be considered restored
▸ "cee" and "tee" are missing the same word
▸ "tal" and "iric" are missing the other word
▸ The missing words are opposites of one another
▸ The title is missing one of the words
▸ "unicial" = unofficial

(2) THE AZ OF THE US

▸ What must be voided? There are two ways to answer that
▸ Voiding letters from the names of states is a good start
▸ "Hawaii" = HI
▸ You will need the two-letter abbreviations for each state
▸ The letters V, O, I, D, E, and D should be replaced with something usually found in equations
▸ The letters V, O, I, D, E, and D should be replaced with certain numbers...
▸ ... according to their position in the alphabet
▸ HI + 22 = DE
▸ What could "+ 22" mean?
▸ It means "move forwards by 22," in this case
▸ You will need to use a Caesar shift for these equations
▸ The letters HI, shifted forwards by 22, become DE

③ SMILE AND WAVE

- ▶ What sort of encoding of a message might be viewed from two different directions?
- ▶ Something shown physically, which would look different from behind
- ▶ Such as a message conveyed using waving, as per the title
- ▶ The code is semaphore
- ▶ How would the semaphore for each word read if viewed from behind?

④ SQUARE ROUTES®

- ▶ The two shaded cells containing asterisks must be the starting cells for OUTSMARTS and ENIGMA
- ▶ There is only one of these shaded cells which has an adjacent vowel, so this must be where OUTSMARTS goes. You now know where the E of ENIGMA goes
- ▶ There are only two other cells where vowels are adjacent, which must be the IU of GENIUS, so you can deduce where most of this word has to go
- ▶ There are seven words but only six start cells, so either GENIUS and GERMAN, or MATHS and MACHINE must share a starting cell

⑤ ODIOUS CONNECTION

- ▶ Why might the clues be grouped together in this way?
- ▶ Once you have solved the clues, try reading them aloud
- ▶ You are looking for a collection of subjects of a certain type of poem
- ▶ Each line describes the subject of an ode (as clued by "odious")

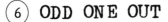

⑥ ODD ONE OUT

▶ The hint here is in the phrase "a little deduction."
▶ It's possible to deduct one letter from each word, leaving another word in each case. What do you notice about the resulting words in comparison to the original words?
▶ Take note of the letters you have deducted

⑦ ANCIENT EQUATIONS

▶ Try writing some numbers out in words
▶ Which "Ancient Equations" might have been written out with letters, not numbers?
▶ Taking 2 from either side of 7 leaves "v"
▶ Do any new numbers emerge when you write the numbers out in words?
▶ Write out the numbers on the right of each equation in words, and then take the given number of letters away from each "side" of the words
▶ What letters are left in the middle?
▶ You are looking for Roman numerals

⑧ A SILVER SPOON

▶ The clues all describe a humorous transition
▶ What might "spoon" in the title hint at?
▶ The solutions to the two clues in each pair are similar, but something has been switched

⑨ COVER VERSIONS

▶ Read the first sentence carefully, and consider what the word "covered" literally means

▶ Is it the songs themselves that have been "covered"… or could it be the artists originally associated with them?

▶ Identify as many of the original artists as you can. Some are easy, e.g. "Mamma Mia" – ABBA

▶ Now look closely at the group names on the right. What do you see in the letters of e.g. BLACK SABBATH?

▶ All of the original artists are hidden inside the names of the groups

▶ Two of the groups need to be joined together

⑩ A NOVEL APPROACH

▶ Where are the different books in the list set?

▶ What might this indicate about how the books were written?

▶ What specific knowledge might you need to read the books as they were originally released?

⑪ ANOTHER GIRL

▶ This puzzle has a musical theme, as suggested by the prompt

▶ Can you think of songs which feature these names?

▶ The title is an example song

▶ All the songs are by the same musical artist

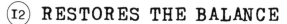

(12) RESTORES THE BALANCE

- ▶ Each item in List C clues one word
- ▶ "Provide insufficient finances" = UNDERFUND
- ▶ In what way does UNDERFUND have a "balance," per the title?
- ▶ "Allure" = ENTICEMENT
- ▶ How can you create ENTICEMENT from the items in Lists A and B?
- ▶ When you have solved the clues in List C, look at the beginning and end of each word
- ▶ They start and end with the same letter strings
- ▶ You will also need to look for anagrams
- ▶ UNDERFUND begins and ends in UND – an anagram of DUN
- ▶ The remaining letters are ERF...
- ▶ ...which is an anagram of REF

(13) VERY THOUGHTFUL

- ▶ Once you have solved the clues, try reading them aloud
- ▶ You are looking for a collection of "thoughtful" individuals

(14) MULTITASKER

- ▶ The words are all anagrams, unique in most cases
- ▶ The words on the right are anagrams of different professions
- ▶ The words on the left are anagrams of the last names of well-known people. There's a one-to-one correspondence between each profession and last name, except one
- ▶ The exception has proven *herself* to be truly exceptional in three of the different professions

(15) CONTROL PANEL

▶ Pay attention to the title
▶ Does it remind you of a computer function?
▶ What function can these particular letters have when used on a computer?
▶ Try combining them with a certain other key
▶ These letters are all used for "ctrl" (or cmd) functions
▶ Replace each letter with the function it performs
▶ Replace "P" with "PRINT"
▶ Replace "X" with "CUT"

(16) MONORAIL OFFENCE

▶ The first station can be found in Paris
▶ You will need to use a certain cipher to decode these names
▶ The first station is Gare Du Nord
▶ The name of the cipher is concealed in the title "Monorail Offence"
▶ The last station is Paddington
▶ All the names are encrypted with the same number of rails
▶ You will need to use a rail fence cipher – look this up if you are not familiar

(17) CULTURAL OMISSIONS

▶ What might be suggested by "cultural"?

▶ One of the lists is made up of novels

▶ Another list is of operas

▶ The first entry in the list is Jane Eyre

▶ Another entry in that same list is Gulliver's Travels – what five letters have been removed in total?

▶ Can you anagram those letters into a word that has something in common with the category the book belongs in?

(18) FIGURE IT OUT

▶ What do the titles of these novels all contain?

▶ "Figure" is a key word in the puzzle title

(19) FUSION CORE

▶ Try replacing the elements with their shorter chemical symbols

▶ Angola and Samoa can be paired up

▶ An element needs to be placed between Angola and Samoa…

▶ …to make another country

▶ One of the hidden countries is Guatemala

▶ Angola + O + Samoa = Laos

(20) CONNOISSEUR OPERATION

▶ You could fly to all of the places in List A

▶ List B contains anagrams

▶ All of the anagrams are linguistically inclined

▶ Items in List C are missing certain letters…

▶ …and perhaps they could be exchanged at a bank?

▶ List D gives you the measure of a man…

▶ …or rather, four men

21 DOPPELGÄNGERS

▶ Try changing the numbers into letters
▶ Assume that A = 1, B = 2, etc – but then what happens?
▶ The fifth word in the list is GRILL
▶ What is a "doppelgänger"?

22 CREATURE COMFORTS

▶ What might "creature comforts" refer to?
▶ The first abbreviated song is by Kate Bush
▶ The second abbreviated song is by Nicki Minaj

23 STREPTOCOCCAL INFECTION

▶ The first song listed is "Bad Blood" by Taylor Swift
▶ What sort of infection might a "streptococcal" infection be?
▶ It might be scarlet fever
▶ How does this connect to the song titles?

24 FAMILIAR CONNECTIONS

▶ The connection is to do with family
▶ All of the people listed share something with one of their parents
▶ A two-letter abbreviation at the end of some of the names might help you

(25) VALUABLE FLOWERS

▶ Different types of letter have been assigned different values here
▶ The value of each type of letter is the same throughout the puzzle
▶ Consonants have exactly double the value of vowels
▶ The word "UP" would have a value of 3 using the same system
▶ Are there any flowers in the puzzle which have the same value as the number you reach when adding the totals of the final two flowers together?

(26) CONTINENTAL DISCOVERIES

▶ Is each line roughly the same length? Why might that be?
▶ Do you have the complete alphabet on each line?
▶ What's missing?
▶ Try rearranging the missing letters
▶ What do all of the entries in the list have in common?
▶ Where are they all located, except for one?

(27) RIGGED

▶ What can be "rigged"?
▶ All of the answers are fictional
▶ The answers could be said to form a fleet

(28) VEXILLOLOGICAL VEXATION

▶ What code uses flags to send messages?
▶ All of the coded names are flags
▶ One of the flags is the Union Jack
▶ Semaphore is the code that uses flags, but you don't need semaphore itself
▶ "SEMAPHORE" is the key you need...
▶ ...for a keyword cipher

Solutions

Every puzzle has not just
a solution, but also an
explanation — not just *what*
is the answer, but *why* is it
the answer? Indeed, for many
puzzles if you can't work
out what to do, and the hints
haven't helped, then try
reading just the first part of
the solution for an explanation
of what's going on, and then
return and solve the original
puzzle armed with the knowledge
of what to do!

ⓘ PATH-OLOGY

Each describes something of a particular quantity, so can be solved as regular mathematical equations:

- ▶ 12 = Little pigs (3) + Players on a baseball team (9)
- ▶ 20 = Quantity of Beatles (4) × Pillars of Islam (5)
- ▶ 39 = US drinking age (21) + Digits of a hand (5) + Cards in a standard suit (13)
- ▶ 19 = Days in a week (7) + Apostles (12)
- ▶ 48 = Harry Potter films (8) + Thieves Ali Baba faced (40)
- ▶ 12 = Ugly sisters (2) + Christian commandments (10)

Each solution can then be matched to an item of the same value in the picture. The numbers in the picture are:

- ▶ Seventh prime: 17
- ▶ Contiguous US states: 48
- ▶ Twilight novels: 4
- ▶ Musketeers: 3
- ▶ Buchan's steps: 39
- ▶ Numbers on a dartboard: 20
- ▶ Noble gases: 6
- ▶ Days of Christmas: 12
- ▶ Adele's debut: 19
- ▶ Horsemen of the Apocalypse: 4

Tracing a path between the items which give the correct answer to each of these equations, in the order in which they appear, creates a star. A "star" is a shape which is one letter short of "start" – the place where you began.

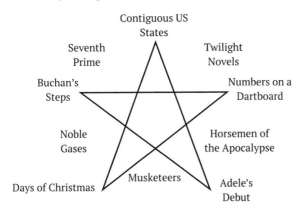

② ALMOST HOME

The right-hand column clues words that are formed by spelling the words clued by the left-hand column backwards, excluding the first letter. In order, the solutions are:

Native – Evita

Deliver – Revile

Ballets – Stella

Petal – Late

Gratis – Sitar

Debut – Tube

③ END-TO-END ENCRYPTION

The instruction is "unlock various codes."

In each line, the final letter of one word is the same as first letter of the next word, e.g. "unbeaten" ends in "N," which is the first letter of "natural."

When all of the "end-to-end" letters are highlighted – including the first letter of the first word in each sentence, and the final letter of the final word – the following words emerge:

UnbeateNaturaLimoncellOrganiCraftworK – or, U N L O C K

VodkAdjudicatoReikImpresariOahUS – or, V A R I O U S

CappuccinOccasioneDelicatEasefulnesS – or, C O D E S

④ LONG NIGHTS

Asunder, outsung, tsunami, or any other word concealing "sun."

Each word in the list conceals a three-letter abbreviation for a day of the week – the title "Long Nights" implies that "short days" will be present. The abbreviations are as follows:

al<u>mon</u>d = Monday
sta<u>tue</u>sque = Tuesday
s<u>wed</u>e = Wednesday
post<u>hu</u>mous = Thursday
un<u>fri</u>end = Friday
er<u>sat</u>z = Saturday

The next word in the list, therefore, should feature "sun," for Sunday.

(5) READY, STEADY...

The clues in column A describe words which contain the word "go." Column B describes words which are created when "go" is removed from the words in column A. In this way the pairs are as follows, given in the order of column A:

"Godot" and "dot" (round mark)

"Wagon" and "wan" (pale of complexion)

"Tango" and "tan" (convert to leather)

"Cargo" and "car" (motor vehicle)

"Flagon" and "flan" (dessert with a sponge base)

(6) SYMBOLISM

Fifty. The numbers refer to the quantity of stars on the flags of the countries referenced.

(7) ACTION!

They are all film titles in which the name of an animal has been replaced by a respective collective noun for that animal:

- ▶ *Four Lions* (2010)
- ▶ *Planet of the Apes* (1968)
- ▶ *Reservoir Dogs* (1992)
- ▶ *Catwoman* (2004)
- ▶ *Fish Tank* (2009)
- ▶ *The Silence of the Lambs* (1991)

⑧ HIGH STATUS

The clues describe different army ranks, which can be ordered from highest to lowest as follows, considering all officers superior to non-commissioned officers: "General" (widespread), "Major" (bright musical key), "Captain" (sports-team leader), "Corporal" (relating to the body), "Private" (not public).

⑨ CHARGED PARTICLES

The clues in column A define words that contain the letters "ion." The clues in column B define the same words with "ion" removed. In order of column A:

"Billion" becomes "bill" (bird's beak)

"Stationed" becomes "stated" (clearly expressed)

"National" becomes "natal" (concerning birth)

"Pioneer" becomes "peer" (social equal)

"Pension" becomes "pens" (writing implements)

"Portion" becomes "port" (place with a dock)

"Lioness" becomes "less" (not as much)

(10) FOUR-WAY JUNCTION

The words can all be sorted into groups based on the hidden direction in each word, one of "up," "down," "left," or "right":

Up:

cupboard

e**up**horia

gro**up**

Left:

c**left**

copy**left**

leftovers

Down:

count**down**

download

lan**down**er

Right:

b**right**

cartw**right**

frighten

(11) SAY AGAIN?

They can all be repeated to make a commonly used phrase:

▶ There, there
▶ Hear! Hear!
▶ Fifty-fifty
▶ Knock knock
▶ Now now

(12) NEOLOGISMS

The paragraph includes several words that were added to the Oxford English Dictionary in January 2020: "bridge-burning," "onboarding," "Brightonian," "hench," and "macaron." Therefore prior to this date these words could not have been "fully approved" by it. (Note that the Oxford Dictionary of English, a completely separate dictionary, did however contain some of these words prior to this date).

(13) MIRROR MIRROR

REPAID, KNITS, REVEL, REWARD, STOPS, and KEELS

Although each pair contains two words that are anagrams of one another, only one of them also spells a word when reversed. In each pair the "reflective" words are therefore:

REPAID, which is "DIAPER" when reversed

KNITS, which is "STINK" when reversed

REVEL, which is "LEVER" when reversed

REWARD, which is "DRAWER" when reversed

STOPS, which is "SPOTS" when reversed

KEELS, which is "SLEEK" when reversed

(14) MISSPENT?

They all end in words for young people, as hinted at by the title "misspent," which can often be followed by "youth":

▶ Clad
▶ Bison
▶ Tallboy
▶ Skid
▶ Canteen
▶ Class

(15) A BRIGHT FUTURE

The equations are made up of things with a certain predominant hue. When they are added together, they produce a hue that would result if they were mixed together as paint. In order, the hues in the equations are:

▶ Yellow + blue = green
▶ Red + blue = purple
▶ Yellow + red = orange
▶ Blue + yellow = green

Given that cherry = red and lemon = yellow, the answer to the final question could be any orange object, so a carrot, for example, or a pumpkin.

(16) ROLL UP

10.   BAGEL + B

11.   SCONE + U

12.   LOAF + T

13.   BROWNIE + T

14.   BRIOCHE + E

15.   CAKE + R

In order, the extra letters are B, U, T, T, E, and R, spelling BUTTER.

(17) IN SHORT

The clues all describe things which have two-letter abbreviations. In order, they describe:

- Pint (PT)
- Afternoon (PM)
- Western Australia (WA)
- Panama (PA)
- Personal Assistant (PA)
- Platinum (PT)
- Washington (WA)
- Prime Minister (PM)

They can be organized into pairs based on their shared abbreviation:

- PA: "Panama" and "personal assistant"
- PM: "Afternoon" and "Prime Minister"
- PT: "Pint" and "platinum"
- WA: "Washington" and "Western Australia"

(18) SEASONING REQUIRED

They all describe the titles of well-known Christmas carols:

- While Shepherds Watched Their Flocks by Night
- The Holly and the Ivy
- We Three Kings
- I Saw Three Ships
- Good King Wenceslas

(19) SINGLES BAR

They were all released by artists known by a single-word name. In order, the artists are:

- ▶ Shakira
- ▶ Rihanna
- ▶ Adele
- ▶ Madonna
- ▶ Cher
- ▶ Sting
- ▶ Morrissey

(20) PHRASE BOOK

Each clue describes a single word. These words can be combined into six common three-word phrases by placing "the" between them.

In the order given, the clues describe "beans," "below," "dust," "belt," "fool," "fly," "spill," "play," "pull," "nest," "bite," and "plug." These can be combined to make the following phrases:

- ▶ Spill the beans
- ▶ Below the belt
- ▶ Bite the dust
- ▶ Fly the nest
- ▶ Play the fool
- ▶ Pull the plug

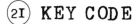

(21) KEY CODE

Each letter has been substituted with a number, with the numbers following the order in which the letters appear on a standard keyboard, reading across the rows from left to right, top to bottom, as follows:

Q	W	E	R	T	Y	U	I	O	P	A	S	D	F	G	H	J	K	L	Z	X	C	V	B	N	M
1	2	3	4	5	6	7	8	9	10	11	12	13	14	15	16	17	18	19	20	21	22	23	24	25	26

Decoded via this cipher, the mathematicians are:

▶ PIERRE DE FERMAT
▶ ISAAC NEWTON
▶ EUCLID
▶ LEONHARD EULER
▶ SOPHIE GERMAIN
▶ PYTHAGORAS

(22) CHECKMATE

Four people from the list have the last name "Black," the other four have the last name "White." In order, the people described are:

▶ Jack White
▶ Jacob Black
▶ Jack Black
▶ Snow White
▶ Barry White
▶ Cilla Black
▶ E.B. White
▶ Sirius Black

(23) TWO WAYS

All four pairs of definitions form a pair of palindromes, ignoring punctuation in the first pair:

- PUPILS
- SLIP-UP

- STRAW
- WARTS

- DELIVER
- REVILED

- LIVE
- EVIL

- STRESSED
- DESSERTS

(24) SPIN THE WHEEL

The words are SAFE, SCAM, SELF, SICK, SHED, SKIM, SMOG, and STAY.

(25) IN A BIND

The names of two knots have in each case been combined by taking alternate letters from each word. LOOP and BEND, for example, could be combined as LEOD or BONP. You must "untangle" them.

The untangled knots are:

RLEP – REEF and SLIP

HHTMH – HITCH and THUMB

FOEBCE – FRENCH and DOUBLE

BIWDIOE – BOWLINE and WINDSOR

GQAANE – GRANNY and SQUARE

(26) MUCH TO DO

"Much Ado About Nothing."

The words situated around the "O" – or, situated "about nothing" – can all be completed by adding much "ado":

me + ado +w = meadow   aficion + ado = aficionado

torn + ado = tornado   ado + lescent = adolescent

sh + ado + w = shadow   re + ado + ut = readout

(27) LINE UP

A water-bearer, as Aquarius follows Capricorn in the zodiac.

(28) ROUND TRIP

The missing letters in each column can be chosen to form three words which create a circular "link word" puzzle, as follows:

(T)Error	(P)Alms	(M)Angling
(I)Con	(I)Rises	(E)Spouse
(M)Ailing	(E)Lope	(A)Cute
(E)Bony	(C)Able	(L)Imp
	(E)Quality	

The three columns therefore spell with their first letters, in turn, TIME, PIECE, and MEAL. Each can be connected to the following word, in a circular fashion, to form a new word: TIMEPIECE, PIECEMEAL, and (circularly) MEALTIME.

(29) SKIING IS THE OTHER WAY

Haar, aardvark, or any other word with a double "a."

Each word in the list contains a set of double letters, where each pair is one position further up the alphabet than that previous pair:

with**h**eld	swa**dd**led
bedra**gg**led	a**cc**ountability
gra**ff**itied	ca**bb**ages
mouth**f**eel	

The next word should therefore contain two consecutive "a"s. The title "Skiing is the Other Way" conversely gives an example of a word that could go at the top of the list, namely "skiing" with its double "i."

(30) A DANCING DILEMMA

The word POINTE. "En pointe" is a method of dancing on the tips of the toes in ballet. The "positions" indicate which letter to take from the title of each ballet, giving the letters I, O, E, P, T, and N in turn. "Order not finalized" suggests an anagram, and these letters can be rearranged to form "pointe."

(31) AURIC ADVANTAGE

Top: Famous "Andy"s (Andy Warhol, Andy Crosby, Andy Murray, Andy Roddick)

Bottom left: Olympic Gold Medallists (Andy Crosby, Andy Murray, Rafael Nadal, Michael Phelps)

Bottom right: Tennis players (Andy Murray, Andy Roddick, Rafael Nadal, Pete Sampras)

"Auric" in the title clues "gold" (hinting at the medals) and "advantage" is a clue for tennis.

(32) SPECIAL OCCASIONS

The materials referenced are the traditional names for certain anniversaries – "gold" represents 50 years, for example. Following this, the numbers in each equation are as follows:

▶ $5^2 = 25$
▶ $50 - 30 = 20$
▶ $5 \times 3 = 15$
▶ $45 - 30 = 15$

"Crystal" would be the appropriate material for the final equation.

(33) TANGLED DUOS

One book from the Old Testament and one from the New Testament are intermixed in each pair. In turn:

GENESIS and MATTHEW

EXODUS and ROMANS

LEVITICUS and EPHESIANS

NUMBERS and TIMOTHY

DEUTERONOMY and CORINTHIANS

RUTH and LUKE

CHRONICLES and REVELATION

JONAH and TITUS

(34) RACKETS

All of the words have animal noises concealed within them. The noises are underlined below:

▶ Home<u>work</u>
▶ Em<u>bark</u>ed
▶ Pre<u>coo</u>ked
▶ S<u>purr</u>ing
▶ Micro<u>array</u>
▶ Un<u>moo</u>ring

(35) BOARD GAME

Opportunity. All of the other words listed can be typed using only the top line of a QWERTY keyboard, while "opportunity" requires you to use one letter from the bottom line, "N."

```
-----------------------------------------------
```
SOLUTIONS FOR LEVEL 2:
META MYSTERIES
```
-----------------------------------------------
```

(I) BOUNDARY CROSSINGS

The United States. Each phrase crosses a state boundary. The final two letters of the first word and the first two letters of the second word in each phrase provide two different standard US state abbreviations. In each phrase, the two states referenced share a border, hence the title of the puzzle.

The bordering states are as follows:

Toga alarm: Georgia (GA) and Alabama (AL)

Sinewy necks: Wyoming (WY) and Nebraska (NE)

Funny pastime: New York (NY) and Pennsylvania (PA)

Pharaoh indigestion: Ohio (OH) and Indiana (IN)

Pilgrims laugh: Mississippi (MS) and Louisiana (LA)

Kiwi mnemonics: Wisconsin (WI) and Minnesota (MN)

Junior waffler: Oregon (OR) and Washington (WA)

(2) A SHARP TASTE

The letters indicated by the musical notes have been used to conceal words. In music, any note with a ♭ (or "flat") symbol indicates that the note one semitone lower than the one indicated by the letter is the one which must be played. Conversely, a ♯ (or "sharp") symbol indicates that a note one semitone higher than the one indicated by the letter is the one which must be played. There is only one semitone difference between the notes B and C (which is why there is no black key between them on a piano keyboard), and similarly the notes E and F. For example, B♯ indicates the same pitch as C. This also means that C♭ is the same pitch as B; E♯ as F; and F♭ as E. In the given tunes, then, the following note-to-letter decryption should be made:

A = A (no change)	F♭ = E
C♭ = B	E♯ = F
B♯ = C	G = G (no change)
D = D (no change)	

With the above applied, the following words are spelled out on each row in turn:

DEFACED	BAGGAGE
CABBAGE	ACCEDED
EFFACED	

The puzzle asks which tune is good enough to eat. Since CABBAGE is the only edible substance spelled out, then the "edible" tune must be B♯ A C♭ C♭ A G F♭ .

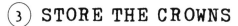

③ STORE THE CROWNS

The letters in the phrase "the crowns" must be placed in the grid, as suggested by the title "Store the Crowns."

The synonyms of each item to be placed in the grid are as follows:

Stop = REST	Play = SHOW
Copy = ECHO	Settlement = TOWN

Each word must appear twice, as required by the instructions, and can be fitted together as follows:

R	E	S	T
E	C	H	O
S	H	O	W
T	O	W	N

④ MAKE THE CALL

The United Kingdom. The equations can be fulfilled by replacing each country with their calling code number, as indicated by the title of the puzzle. The correct numbers are as follows:

France (33) + Australia (61) = Sri Lanka (94)

Germany (49) + Russia (7) = Chile (56)

Egypt (20) + Belgium (32) = Mexico (52)

South Africa (27) + New Zealand (64) = India (91)

Norway (47) + Spain (34) = Japan (81)

The area codes for Austria and the USA are +43 and +1

(5) HANDS ON HEARTS

The United Kingdom. The national anthem "God Save the Queen" is hidden with one of each of its words concealed in each phrase:

- ▶ Indi**go** dye
- ▶ Sal**sa ve**rde
- ▶ Faint-h**earte**d
- ▶ Obli**que en**clave

(6) ON TOP OF THINGS

"OVER" is the connecting word, as it can be placed before the solution to each anagram to make a new word. In order, the restored words are:

- ▶ RIPE (making OVERRIPE)
- ▶ EAGER (making OVEREAGER)
- ▶ TONES (making OVERTONES)
- ▶ RULES (making OVERRULES)
- ▶ SHOOT (making OVERSHOOT)
- ▶ SHARE (making OVERSHARE)

⑦ ESPIONAGE GENERATOR

Each of the clues can be solved as follows:

List A	List B	List C
Automobile = CAR	Argument = ROW	Attempt = TRY
Because = FOR	Enclosure = PEN	Fox's home = DEN
Male swan = COB	Male progeny = SON	Place to sleep = BED
Scam = CON	Network = WEB	Plump = FAT
Spoil = MAR	Obtained = GOT	Small insect = ANT
Wager = BET	Pole = ROD	Two fives = TEN

Each of these three-letter words can be combined to create one of the clues in the "Results" list:

Results

Covered in spider silk	= COB+WEB+BED = cobwebbed
Harmonious	= CON+SON+ANT = consonant
Large pea variety	= MAR+ROW+FAT = marrowfat
Neglected	= FOR+GOT+TEN = forgotten
Walked upon	= BET+ROD+DEN = betrodden
Woodwork	= CAR+PEN+TRY = carpentry

The title "Espionage Generator" contains two more examples of words which can be created in a similar way: "ESP+ION+AGE" and "GEN+ERA+TOR."

⑧ ACTS UP

The clues are all quotations from Shakespeare's *Hamlet*, which appear in different acts and scenes of the play:

- ▶ "This bodes some strange eruption to our state" (Act 1, Scene 1)
- ▶ "Frailty, thy name is Woman" (Act 1, Scene 2)
- ▶ "To thine own self be true" (Act 1, Scene 3)
- ▶ "Something is rotten in the state of Denmark" (Act 1, Scene 4)
- ▶ "By indirections find directions out" (Act 2, Scene 1)
- ▶ "To be or not to be" (Act 3, Scene 1)
- ▶ "The lady doth protest too much" (Act 3, Scene 2)
- ▶ "Words without thoughts never to heaven go" (Act 3, Scene 3)
- ▶ "Alas, how shall this bloody deed be answer'd?" (Act 4, Scene 1)
- ▶ "Alas, poor Yorick. I knew him, Horatio" (Act 5, Scene 1)

The act and scene number can be used as coordinates, with the act as the vertical coordinate (per the title "Acts Up"). Shade the grid with these coordinates to reveal a letter "F," the initial of Fortinbras, a minor character in Hamlet who has the final line in the play:

	1	2	3	4	5
1	■	■	■	■	
2	■				
3	■	■	■		
4	■				
5	■				

(9) FICTITIOUS DIFFICULTY

The titles in this list have been manipulated by removing all vowels and spaces, then writing all remaining letters in reverse order. In order, the books are:

▶ SENSE AND SENSIBILITY
▶ PRIDE AND PREJUDICE
▶ EMMA
▶ MANSFIELD PARK
▶ WUTHERING HEIGHTS
▶ PERSUASION

Wuthering Heights is the only book in this list not by Jane Austen, making it the odd one out. The author is Emily Brontë, whose name would be TNRBYLM using the same coding system.

(10) BEST FRIENDS

They are all descriptions of words which are also breeds of dog. In order, they are:

▶ Greyhound
▶ Boxer
▶ Husky
▶ Pointer
▶ Kelpie

⑪ LOOK AGAIN

Each of the words listed can be divided into two separate words, and then "double" can be added before each of these separate words to form two new words or phrases:

▶ Double take and double over
▶ Double down and double time
▶ Double lock and double up
▶ Double-cross and double-check
▶ Double back and double-date
▶ Double play and double room

⑫ TITLE CONFUSION

The word "day" has been replaced by a different time of day in each instance. In order, the original titles are:

▶ "A Day in the Life" (song by The Beatles)
▶ "One Fine Day" (song by The Chiffons)
▶ *Die Another Day* (2002 film)
▶ "A Hard Day's Night" (song by The Beatles)
▶ "Beautiful Day" (song by U2)
▶ *The Day After Tomorrow* (2004 film)

⑬ EYE LEVEL

Left set: words that are palindromes

Right set: words that were created as abbreviations of longer names (e.g. SONAR is derived from "SOund Navigation and Ranging")

Intersection: words that are both

(14) HYDRATION

"Parisian water" is the French word for water, "eau," which is pronounced "oh." The solutions to each clue can each have an "oh" sound added to the end to create new words:

▶ Furl + oh = furlough

▶ Soured + oh = sourdough

▶ Disk + oh = disco

▶ Oars + oh = orzo

▶ Gust + oh = gusto

▶ Band + oh = bandeau

(15) NICE TO SEE YOU

They are all descriptions of French terms used in English. In order, they are:

▶ Cliché

▶ Cul-de-sac

▶ Déjà vu

▶ Matinee

▶ Chauffeur

▶ Femme fatale

(16) ORCHESTRAL PUZZLE

One letter can be changed in each of the instruments to make the words described by the clues

"Harp" can become "carp" or "hare"

"Tuba" can become "tuna" or "Cuba"

"Cello" can become "hello" or "cells"

"Horn" can become "worn" or "corn"

"Trumpet" can become "crumpet"

Following this rule, "flute" could become, for example, "a chance happening" (fluke) or "a channel for conveying water" (flume).

(17) SETT ASIDE

An ant.

Each of the items in the list contains the name of an animal surrounded by the name of its home. FOHARERM, for example, contains HARE, surrounded by its home, FORM. The title "Sett Aside" is a clue to this mechanism, as a sett is a badger's home, and the words can be considered to be "aside" their inhabitants.

The full animal and home combinations are as follows:

BIWASPKE = WASP in BIKE (an archaic term for a wasp's nest)

FOHARERM = HARE in FORM   KENDOGNEL = DOG in KENNEL

NEOWLST = OWL in NEST   SPIGTY = PIG in STY

COHENOP = HEN in COOP   HIBEEVE = BEE in HIVE

HOOTTERLT = OTTER in HOLT   DELIONN = LION in DEN

A FORMICARY is an ants' nest but, in this list, does not contain an ANT. The answer to "who's not home," therefore, is an ant.

(18) FIRST FIRSTS

Taking the first letter of each word in the three bullet points spells out the first line of three well-known novels, disregarding spaces and punctuation. The three first lines are as follows, with the novels they open (their "sources") shown in brackets:

▶ Call me Ishmael (*Moby Dick* by Herman Melville)
▶ It was a pleasure to burn (*Fahrenheit 451* by Ray Bradbury)
▶ All children, except one, grow up (*Peter Pan* by J.M. Barrie)

⑲ IN ANOTHER TECHNICAL AREA

ARN. The three-letter codes are the IATA airport codes for the airports serving the capital city of each country. ARN is the code for Stockholm Arlanda Airport.

"IATA" is clued by the initials in the title: "**I**n **A**nother **T**echnical **A**rea."

⑳ ABSENCES

A set of trees have lost their LEAVES, which is also clued by the title, "Absences."

Each of the first seven lines conceals the name of a deciduous tree, with the letters of the word "LEAVES" removed.
IR MP = SILVER MAPLE
ONDON PN = LONDON PLANE
WID ERIC = WILD SERVICE
Y OK = VALLEY OAK
DR = ALDER/ELDER
DR = ELDER/ALDER
M = ELM

㉑ YOU'VE GOT MAIL

Each of the solutions to the clues ends with "man." In order, the clues describe

▶ Caiman
▶ Batman
▶ German
▶ Ottoman
▶ (Harry S.) Truman

(22) LETTER OPENING

Each clue describes a word which, when said out loud, sounds like a single letter of the alphabet. The two sets consist of four words each. The words in the first set begin with the letter they sound like (hence the puzzle title, "letter openings"), while the words in the second set begin with a different letter to the one they sound like. The two sets are as follows:

- ▶ B – Bee (hive-dwelling insect)
- ▶ J – Jay (a decorative member of the crow family)
- ▶ O – Owe (have a need to repay)
- ▶ P – Pea (small green vegetable)

- ▶ C – Sea (expanse of water)
- ▶ I – Eye (visual organ)
- ▶ U – Ewe (a female sheep)
- ▶ Y – Why (for what purpose?)

(23) COOPED UP

A group of animals – in order, the words missing from the spaces are as follows:

- ▶ CATCALL
- ▶ DOGWOOD
- ▶ PIGTAILS
- ▶ FISHWIFE
- ▶ COWLICK
- ▶ HORSEPLAY

- - · — — — · — · — — · — — — — · — — · · ·

24 ROUND BRITAIN TOUR

The places are all anagrams of ONE, TWO, THREE etc, with the same number of letters left over (eg, ETON = ONE + 1 left over)

HIGHER DINTING satisfies EIGHT + 8 letters left over, NINE + 9, and TEN + 10.

25 HIDDEN CONNECTIONS

Each word in the four numbered sets has a different short word concealed within it – for example, TENT is hidden in ATTENTION. The five words in each set are connected by a theme. In order, the themes are 4-letter countries, types of tree, types of fish, and types of fruit. Each hidden word is underlined below:

1. 4-letter countries: S<u>CHAD</u>ENFREUDE, ASP<u>IRAN</u>TS, EGO<u>MANI</u>AC, IN<u>CUBA</u>TION, HESP<u>ERUS</u>

2. Types of tree: GUN<u>FIR</u>E, CL<u>OAK</u>ED, H<u>ELM</u>ET, HAPP<u>INES</u>S, FACE<u>PALM</u>ING

3. Types of fish: ES<u>CARP</u>MENT, S<u>PIKE</u>D, FREE<u>LOA</u>DER, EN<u>COD</u>ING, T<u>UNA</u>BLE

4. Types of fruit: SUB<u>LIME</u>LY, AP<u>PEAR</u>ING, SE<u>DATE</u>D, EF<u>FIG</u>Y, GR<u>APPLE</u>R

26 REMORSE ON THE RADIO

Morse code, and a mirror.

Lists 1 and 2 both contain code words from the NATO phonetic alphabet ("on the radio"). When the single letters indicated by the code words in both List 1 and List 2 are written out in Morse code (clued via "Remorse") they appear as follows, in the order given:

List 1		List 2	
G =	- - ·	W =	· - -
U =	· · -	D =	- · ·
L =	· - · ·	F =	· · · - ·
A =	· -	N =	- ·
Q =	- - · -	Y =	- · - -
V =	· · · -	B =	- · · ·

The Morse code in List 1 is an exact mirror image of the code in List 2. The Morse in List 2 has then been converted back to the appropriate NATO code words.

(27) KNOW-ALLS

They are all descriptions of song titles recorded by Beyoncé. In order, the songs are:

▶ "Flawless"
▶ "Green Light"
▶ "Formation"
▶ "Halo"
▶ "Freedom"
▶ "Irreplaceable"

28 STORE THE CROWNS

The letters in the phrase "the crowns" must be placed in the grid, as suggested by the title "Store the Crowns."

The synonyms of each item to be placed in the grid are as follows:

Stop = REST   Play = SHOW

Copy = ECHO   Settlement = TOWN

Each word must appear twice, as required by the instructions, and can be fitted together as follows:

R	E	S	T
E	C	H	O
S	H	O	W
T	O	W	N

29 MARRIAGE THERAPY

Middleton, Deneuve, or anyone else named "Catherine." The last names listed all belong to well-known people who share their first names with Henry VIII's six wives. His final wife was Catherine Parr. They are listed in the order in which the historical figures whose name they share were married to Henry VIII:

▶ Catherine Zeta-Jones (Catherine of Aragon)
▶ Anne Frank (Anne Boleyn)
▶ Jane Fonda (Jane Seymour)
▶ Anne Hathaway (Anne of Cleves)
▶ Catherine Tate (Catherine Howard)
▶ E.g. Catherine Middleton (Catherine Parr)

(30) SCIENTIFIC STATES

Nebraska is 10. The two-letter abbreviation of each state is the same as the two-letter abbreviation for the element which corresponds to the number next to it in the list.

Arkansas, AR – Argon, Ar, 18
California, CA – Calcium, Ca, 20
Colorado, CO – Cobalt, Co, 27
Georgia, GA – Gallium, Ga, 31
Indiana, IN – Indium, In, 49
Minnesota, MN – Manganese, Mn, 25
Nebraska, NE – Neon, Ne, 10

(31) BUILD YOUR OWN PALINDROME I

The answers in alphabetical order are: ETNA, GALLIVANT, MOSELLE, SEMITE, SOMETIMES, TAGLIATELLE, TAILGATE, VILLAGE.

The palindrome they form is: SEMITE, MOSELLE, TAILGATE, GALLIVANT, ETNA, VILLAGE, TAGLIATELLE, SOMETIMES.

(32) SLOOP POOLS

The words are STUB, SWAP, SPAN, STEW, SLAP, SMUG, STAR, and STUN.

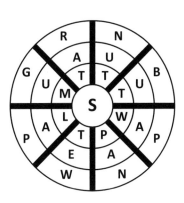

When read backwards, the words are BUTS, PAWS, NAPS ,WETS, PALS, GUMS, RATS, and NUTS.

① TYPECAST

The question is "WHY." The letters in the puzzle indicate paths that can be traced between keys on a standard QWERTY keyboard, which create the shapes of the letters "W," "H," and "Y."

② JOIN THE – DOTS –

The code formed by the equations is "MORSE."

The equations can all be solved by writing each letter or number in Morse code, which is clued by the dashes and "dots" in the title. In each equation, the Morse code for each of the two first figures can be combined as shown to create the third. For example, A + O = 1 becomes:

· –   +   – – –   =   · – – – –

The first set of equations therefore work as follows:

· – (A)	+	– – – (O)	= · – – – – (1)
· · · – (U)	+	– – (M)	= · · – – – (2)
· · (I)	+	· – – (W)	= · · · – – (3)
· · · · (H)	+	– (T)	= · · · · – (4)
· – (A)	+	– (T)	= · – · – (W)

The remaining equations can then be solved in the same way:

– (T)	+	– (T)	= – – (M)
– (T)	+	– – (M)	= – – – (O)
· (E)	+	– · (N)	= · – · (R)
· · (I)	+	· (E)	= · · · (S)
· · (I)	–	· (E)	= · (E)

The solution letters, when read in order, spell MORSE.

(3) ANIMAL CHARACTERS

The animals appear in three different literary works: *Alice's Adventures in Wonderland* by Lewis Carroll, *The Wind in the Willows* by Kenneth Grahame, and *The Jungle Book* by Rudyard Kipling. They can be sorted into three lists as follows, with the character names given in brackets:

▶ *Alice's Adventures in Wonderland*: Cat (the Cheshire Cat), Rabbit (the White Rabbit), Hare (the March Hare), Caterpillar (the Caterpillar)

▶ *The Wind in the Willows*: Water vole (Ratty), Mole (Mole), Toad (Mr Toad), Badger (Mr Badger)

▶ *The Jungle Book:* Wolf (Akela), Tiger (Shere Khan), Black panther (Bagheera), Bear (Baloo)

(4) OUTLINE THE LINEOUT

"Inside Out." Each of the words in the list has either had the word "out" inserted where "in" should be, or "in" inserted where "out" should be, as follows:

sprin = sprout	sinh = south
uncinh = uncouth	moutd = mind
boutgo = bingo	marouta = marina
infox = outfox	joutx = jinx
adoroutg = adoring	sproutg = spring
abin = about	yinh = youth
moutor = minor	loute = line
scined = scouted	snin = snout

Given that every "out" is where an "in" should be, and every "in" is where an "out" should be, you could say that these words have been turned "in-side-out." *Inside Out* is a Disney Pixar animated film released in 2015.

⑤ NAME DROPPING

Harrison Ford would be a good suggestion, or indeed anyone else well-known with the first name "Harrison." The sequence is that the last name of the person becomes the first name of the following person (or the last part of their last name in the case of Lloyd George):

▶ Jack Daniel
▶ Daniel Craig
▶ Craig David
▶ David Lloyd George
▶ George Harrison

⑥ THE ROOT OF THE PROBLEM

The clues are all descriptions of Latin words or phrases used in English. In order, the words and phrases are:

▶ Alibi   ▶ Bonus
▶ Ad nauseam   ▶ Alumnus
▶ Ego   ▶ Vice versa
▶ Campus

⑦ FAMOUS FIGURES

They are all well-known people who share a last name with a former president of the USA. In each instance, the last name of the president has been replaced by his immediate predecessor's:

▶ Marilyn Monroe
▶ Howard Carter
▶ Elizabeth Taylor
▶ George Harrison
▶ Henry Ford
▶ Samuel Johnson

⑧ READ THE SIGNALS

Ship berth 6. The times given in the table correspond to flag positions in semaphore, when the times are represented by the hands on a clock face. The times for each ship berth therefore read as follows:

1. SAIL		16.	KEEL
2. MAST		17.	CAPTAIN
3. RUDDER		18.	DECK
4. BOW		19.	HULL

"Captain" is the odd one out, as it is the only entry in the list which is not a part of a ship.

⑨ ALL THAT GLISTERS

They are all well-known quotations from Shakespeare plays, with the vowels and punctuation removed and spaces rearranged:

▶ Now is the winter of our discontent (*Richard III*)
▶ Ill met by moonlight, proud Titania (*A Midsummer Night's Dream*)
▶ Fair is foul, and foul is fair (*Macbeth*)
▶ Friends, Romans, countrymen, lend me your ears (*Julius Caesar*)
▶ If music be the food of love, play on (*Twelfth Night*)
▶ A pair of star-crossed lovers take their life (*Romeo and Juliet*)

⑩ NOAH'S ARK

The scientific names of the animals listed are all tautonyms, where the same word is used for both genus and species. In order, the scientific names are as follows:

▶ *Rattus rattus*   ▶ *Bison bison*
▶ *Vulpes vulpes*   ▶ *Chinchilla chinchilla*
▶ *Lynx lynx*   ▶ *Cygnus cygnus*

Noah's Ark had two of each animal, just as these names effectively do.

⑪ LEGENDARY CELLS

Top circle: Human body parts (note that the abbreviation "Achilles" can be used as a standalone word to refer to the Achilles tendon)

Bottom-left circle: Flowering plants

Bottom-right circle: Characters in Greek mythology

(12) A BIT FISHY

Several species of fish have been poached.

Each group of letters can be restored by adding back in a missing letter, which has been "poached" from the middle of each:

aChe bOw iDea

eBb goAl aSh aSh

eMu goAl aChe sKi eEl aRc eEl isLe

uPper isLe goAl aIr aChe eEl

aTom aRc bOw bUzz aTom

In each line, the "poached" letters spell out the name of a fish. Therefore COD, BASS, MACKEREL, PLAICE, and TROUT have been "poached" from each line in turn.

(13) NUMBER SEARCH

20. The arrows are instructions to apply to a QWERTY keyboard, where each new line provides the key movement steps to reach the next letter in the solution. Taken in turn, they spell out TWENTY.

"A tool used for golf" clues "tee," a homophone of the letter "T" – this gives you the "T" key as the starting point. From here, move three keys to the left, taking you to "W." Then move one key to the right to reach "E," then two keys down and right, then three to the right to "N," and so on, moving only to adjacent keys at each move.

(14) CHERRY OR PECAN?

The quotation is by Archimedes: "Give me a place to stand, and I will move the earth."

Archimedes' constant is pi, clued by the title of the puzzle as "cherry" and "pecan," which can both be types of pie, a homophone of "pi." The quote can be revealed by using pi to twelve digits as an indicator of which word to take from each sentence. Pi to twelve digits is 3.14159265359, so take the third word from the first sentence, the first word from the second sentence, the fourth from the third sentence, and so on, through until the ninth word from the final sentence.

(15) THE MOVABLE EQUATION

$$2^5 9^2 = 2592$$

(16) CINEMATIC EFFECT

The strings of letters are all rearranged acronyms of episodes of the Star Wars, Harry Potter, and Lord of the Rings film franchises, so can be sorted into three categories according to which franchise they belong to. The films are as follows:

Harry Potter:
- ▶ *The Chamber of Secrets* (TCOS/OSCT)
- ▶ *The Prisoner of Azkaban* (TPOA/PATO)
- ▶ *The Goblet of Fire* (TGOF/FOGT)
- ▶ *The Order of the Phoenix* (TOOTP/POTOT)
- ▶ *The Half-Blood Prince* (THBP/PHBT)

Lord of the Rings:
- *The Fellowship of the Ring* (TFOTR/TOTRF)
- *The Two Towers* (TTT/TTT)
- *The Return of the King* (TROTK/KOTRT)

Star Wars:
- *A New Hope* (ANH/HAN)
- *The Empire Strikes Back* (TESB/BEST)
- *Return of the Jedi* (ROTJ/TROJ)
- *Attack of the Clones* (AOTC/CATO)
- *Revenge of the Sith* (ROTS/SORT or STOR)
- *The Force Awakens* (TFA/AFT)
- *The Rise of Skywalker* (TROS/SORT or STOR)

(17) A CAPITALIST WORLD

Each of their capital cities shares its name with its country, albeit for all but Singapore with the word "City" after it.

(18) SUSTAINED STRUCTURE

Birds.

All letters in the diamond have been replaced with numbers, as follows:

1 = D	6 = R
2 = A	7 = B
3 = G	8 = I
4 = S	9 = C
5 = E	

(19) FAMOUS LINES

They are all examples of "diacope," a rhetorical device where one or more words are repeated, but separated by a different word or phrase. In each instance, the final word or words also appear directly before the first word in each quotation. The repeated elements are underlined:

- ▶ <u>Zed's dead</u>, baby, Zed's dead
- ▶ <u>A horse</u>, a horse! My kingdom for a horse!
- ▶ <u>Stella!</u> Hey Stella!
- ▶ <u>Food</u>, glorious food
- ▶ <u>Put out the light</u>, and then, put out the light

(20) LIGHT, LONG, OR FULL?

The phrases described all contain imperial units of measurement. These phrases can be organized into pairs based on whether the units are used to measure length, weight, or volume:

Length:
- ▶ On the back foot (at a disadvantage)
- ▶ Go the extra mile (make a special effort)

Weight:
- ▶ Stone-cold sober (definitely not drunk)
- ▶ Pound of flesh (Shylock's demand)

Volume
- ▶ Pint-sized (tiny)
- ▶ Ten-gallon hat (cowboy's headgear)

(21) BASIC COMPOSITION

Each "compound" is created using the atomic numbers of chemical elements, which when replaced with their one- or two-letter chemical symbol will spell out words. Using "4 + 18" as an example, 4 is the atomic number of the element Beryllium with chemical symbol Be, and 18 is the atomic number of Argon with chemical symbol Ar. When combined, the two elements spell out "BeAr," or "bear."

When this rule is applied to all the compounds, the following words are produced:

BeAr	MoUSe
CoYOTe	NePAl
IReLaNd	RaCCoON
MoNaCo	SiNGaPoRe

The words can be sorted into two groups – one of animals (bear, coyote, mouse, and raccoon), and one of geographical locations (Ireland, Monaco, Nepal, and Singapore). The appropriate groupings of the compounds as encoded in the puzzle, therefore, is as follows:

Animals:

4 + 18 (BeAr)

27 + 39 + 8 + 52 (CoYOTe)

42 + 92 + 34 (MoUSe)

88 + 6 + 27 + 8 + 7 (RaCCoON)

Locations:

53 + 75 + 57 + 60 (IReLaNd)

42 + 11 + 27 (MoNaCo)

10 + 15 + 13 (NePAl)

14 + 7 + 31 + 84 + 75 (SiNGaPoRe)

(22) STATE MATHEMATICS

Each equation uses clues with solutions that share a certain set of letters. When the letters of the solution to the second clue in each equation are taken away from the letters of the first clue, the answer to the final clue results. You do not need to reorder the letters in the first word, but you do need to do so with the second word, and choose which to eliminate judiciously where there are multiple options.

▶ OKLAHOMA – KOALA = OHM
▶ VERMONT – MONET = VR
▶ DELAWARE – ADELE = WAR

(23) CIRCLE RANGE

Left-hand circle: words of French origin

Right-hand circle: paint hues

"Blue" could be considered the odd one out in the overlap, as the other two hues (orange and violet) have the same spelling in French as in English, whereas the French for blue is "bleu."

The words "Circle" and "Range," found in the title, are also of French origin.

(24) ELEMENTAL PROBLEM

The word "works" can be added to the end of the first three elements to make "fireworks," "waterworks," and "earthworks." However, "works" cannot be added to "air" because "airworks" is not a word, meaning that "air" never "works" – so cannot "be functioning."

(25) ECHO?

You are on the podium, in THIRD position.

Words used in the NATO phonetic alphabet have been encoded using a Caesar shift. Each word has been shifted according to the position of its initial letter (and the letter the whole word indicates, in the NATO alphabet) in the alphabet. For example, the letters in the word ALPHA, which signal the letter "A," would have been shifted forward by 1 place to give BMQIB.

So:

NUHAI is "TANGO" with a shift of 20, as T is in 20th position.

PWBMT is "HOTEL" with a shift of 8, as H is in 8th position.

RWMRJ is "INDIA" with a shift of 9, as I is in 9th position.

JGEWG is "ROMEO" with a shift of 18, as R is in 18th position.

HIPXE is "DELTA" with a shift of 4, as D is in 4th position.

The letters spelled out by the decoded NATO characters are therefore T, H, I, R, and D, indicating that the solver is ranked third, and therefore likely to be on the on the podium.

The NATO phonetic alphabet itself is hinted at by the word "Echo" in the title, and the fictional **N**ational **A**udio **T**ransmission **O**bservatory.

(26) QUITE CONTRARY

All of these words are contranyms, where each word has two meanings that contradict each other:

- ▶ Clip: can mean either to fasten two objects together, or to cut something (and thereby separate it into two objects)
- ▶ Lease: can mean either to grant property or to take property
- ▶ Weather: can mean either to withstand difficult conditions, or to be worn away by exposure to difficult weather conditions
- ▶ Sanction: can mean either a permission for an action, or a penalty for an action
- ▶ Left: can mean either departed or remaining
- ▶ Dust: can mean either to remove a layer of powder, or to cover something with a layer of powder

(27) INTERESTING CHARACTERS

The titles of all of these novels are the name of a character who appears in them. The first names and last names of each have been mixed up, as have those of the authors. The restored novels are as follows:

- ▶ *Agnes Grey* by Anne Brontë
- ▶ *Anna Karenina* by Leo Tolstoy
- ▶ *Robinson Crusoe* by Daniel Defoe
- ▶ *Silas Marner* by George Eliot
- ▶ *Mary Poppins* by P.L. Travers
- ▶ *Jane Eyre* by Charlotte Brontë
- ▶ *Oliver Twist* by Charles Dickens
- ▶ *Tom Jones* by Henry Fielding
- ▶ *Lorna Doone* by R.D. Blackmore

(28) ACROSS THE DEEP BLUE SEA

Bari, Italy to Split, Croatia. All of the other journeys involve journeying across a body of water with a hue in its name. In order, the bodies of water are the Black Sea, the Yellow Sea, the White Sea, the Adriatic Sea, and the Red Sea.

(29) INTERNATIONAL STARS

Either the first name or last name of the people described is also the name of a major city in one of the countries listed in the right-hand column. In order, the people described in the left-hand column, and the country they match with, are as follows. The cities are underlined:

Irving Berlin – Germany

Paris Hilton – France

Jack London – UK

Orlando Bloom – USA

Sofia Coppola – Bulgaria

Florence Nightingale – Italy

(30) AS I WAS SAYING

These are all descriptions of English idioms featuring animals. In order, the clues refer to the following:

▸ The <u>elephant</u> in the room
▸ Let the <u>cat</u> out of the bag
▸ A wild <u>goose</u> chase
▸ The straw that broke the <u>camel</u>'s back
▸ Don't count your <u>chickens</u> before they hatch

(31) ELEVEN OF TWELVE

July – or "JUL" – is missing. The letters that have been removed from each word are abbreviations (the first three letters) for the twelve months of the year. The only month whose abbreviation is not listed is July.

TUR<u>NOV</u>ER (November)   LA<u>UG</u>HTER (August)

LI<u>FEB</u>OAT (February)   DIS<u>MAY</u>ED (May)

UP<u>MAR</u>KET (March)   J<u>AN</u>GLING (January)

HOU<u>SEP</u>LANT (September)   IN<u>JUN</u>CTION (June)

MAL<u>APR</u>OPISM (April)   UN<u>DEC</u>IDED (December)

CONC<u>OCT</u>ION (October)

32 HE-LEXICAL CONUNDRUM

Place the words so they read both inwards and outwards, so each cell is used by two words. The words are:

Inward	Outward
TILES	FOR
OLDEN	PREP
CAMEO	PURE
PLATE	DROP
MAESTRO	MIRES
TERSER	RETORT
IMP	SEA
ORDER	METAL
UPPER	POEM
PROF	ACNED
	LOSE
	LIT

The letters in the shaded cells are I, O, N, M, A, T, M, and E. The "twisted spiral" is an "AMMONITE" – a spiral-shaped fossil formed by anagramming (or making "twisted") the shaded letters.

33 BOUNCE BACK

They all contain tennis terms. The hidden words are underlined below:

- ▶ Pe<u>ace</u>
- ▶ Ro<u>llover</u>
- ▶ Pres<u>erved</u>
- ▶ Un<u>break</u>able
- ▶ Bul<u>let</u>in
- ▶ Liter<u>ally</u>

CONTRARY PAIRS

The pair "canonical ratatouille" is a tourist.

In each of the word pairs, one word conceals the word "yes," and the other the word "no," as follows:

bi<u>no</u>cular e<u>ye</u>sight

spr<u>yes</u>t a<u>no</u>rak

unk<u>no</u>wn d<u>yes</u>

<u>no</u>rmal pol<u>yes</u>ter

s<u>no</u>re goodb<u>yes</u>

In "canonical ratatouille," however, "non" and "oui" are concealed, which are the French words for "no" and "yes" respectively. As such, this pair can be said to be a "tourist" from another language.

VICTORIOUS

The next item in the sequence would be "11 = France." The sequence is winners of the FIFA World Cup in chronological order from 2002, with the sum of the digits in the year of each tournament given:
Brazil in 2002 = 2 + 0 + 0 + 2 = 4
Italy in 2006 = 2 + 0 + 0 + 6 = 8
Spain in 2010 = 2 + 0 + 1 + 0 = 3
Germany in 2014 = 2 + 0 + 1 + 4 = 7
France in 2018 = 2 + 0 + 1 + 8 = 11

WORD CONNECTIONS

They are all English words which derive from Hindi words.

(1) LONERS

They are all 12-letter words that do not have any repeated letters.

(2) SINK OR SWIM

The boats above the surface have lost their "OAR"s – or, they have lost the letters O, A, and R.

The boats below the surface have sunk without a "TRACE" – i.e. they have lost the letters T, R, A, C, and E.

The restored boats, reading from left to right, are:
CANOE – CNE / NO
CATAMARAN – CTMN / MN
CLIPPER – CLIPPE / LIPP
GALLEON – GLLEN / GLLON
NARROWBOAT – NWBT / NOWBO

(3) COUPLES' RETREAT

The odd definition is "Inflatable decoration," clueing "balloon."

Five of the words clued have three sets of double letters, while "balloon" has only two sets. In order, the solutions to the clues are:

▶ Bookkeeper
▶ Tallahassee
▶ Balloon
▶ Mississippi
▶ Committee
▶ Tennessee

④ BESTSELLERS

These clues describe the titles of five globally bestselling albums. In order, the album titles are:

- *Saturday Night Fever* by Bee Gees
- *Rumours* by Fleetwood Mac
- *21* by Adele
- *Bat Out of Hell* by Meat Loaf
- *The Dark Side of the Moon* by Pink Floyd

⑤ EASY PIECES

"Million Dollar Baby" is the odd one out.

The words can be paired up to create the partially complete names of six films, as follows:

card + stud

days + later

dollar + baby

first + dates

inch + chest

jump + street

The film names can all then be completed with a number. The completed names are as follows, in order from smallest to largest value of the added number:

5 Card Stud	*44 Inch Chest*
21 Jump Street	*50 First Dates*
28 Days Later	*Million Dollar Baby*

Million Dollar Baby is the odd one out in the resulting list, as it is the only film to write its number with words rather than digits. The title "Easy Pieces" is referencing the film *Five Easy Pieces*.

⑥ ONE STEP AT A TIME

The instructions generate a word pyramid, where one letter in turn is added to those in the previous word, then rearranged to create a new word. Each word given in the puzzle has been replaced with a clue, as follows:

Gnaw = BITE
Group = TRIBE
Sour = BITTER
Fragile = BRITTLE
Songbook = LIBRETTO

Thus, beginning with "BITE" (clued as "gnaw") and adding R creates "TRIBE," then adding T to "TRIBE" gives "BITTER," and so on.

The completed pyramid is therefore:

BITE

TRIBE

BITTER

BRITTLE

LIBRETTO

⑦ BLACK, NOT WHITE

Restoring the "missing" features of this puzzle forms a set of musical notes (made up of the missing components only, underlined below), which can all be played on the black keys of a piano, as per the title:

ABASEMENT	FRIGHTFUL	MUDFLAT
BLASTING	GLANCE	FLATLINES
CENSURE	FLATBREAD	SHARP-TONGUED
DALLIANCE	FLATFISH	SHARP-EYED
EVALUATION	SHARPSHOOTER	

⑧ HIDE AND SEEK

The US. The names can all be found within the names of states or provinces in the countries indicated:

- ▶ Scot – Nova Scotia (Canada)
- ▶ Brad – Newfoundland and Labrador (Canada)
- ▶ Kat – Saskatchewan (Canada)
- ▶ Bert – Alberta (Canada)
- ▶ Lori – Florida (USA)
- ▶ Diana – Indiana (USA)
- ▶ Sian – Louisiana (USA)
- ▶ Mary – Maryland (USA)
- ▶ Carol – North Carolina or South Carolina (USA)

⑨ CHARACTER REFERENCE

The first names of all the people listed are also the titles of well-known novels. In order, the people described and the novels they share a name with are:

- ▶ Orlando Bloom – *Orlando* by Virginia Woolf
- ▶ Kim Cattrall – *Kim* by Rudyard Kipling
- ▶ Heidi Klum – *Heidi* by Johanna Spyri
- ▶ Matilda of Flanders – *Matilda* by Roald Dahl
- ▶ Carrie Fisher – *Carrie* by Stephen King
- ▶ Ulysses S. Grant – *Ulysses* by James Joyce
- ▶ Rebecca Hall – *Rebecca* by Daphne du Maurier

⑩ NEAT HANDWRITING

When written in lower case, none of these words have any letters with ascenders (for example, "d" or "h"), or descenders (for example, "y" or "g").

(11) LEADING LETTERS

The countries can be sorted into three lists of four countries, each of which has a capital city starting with the same letter:

B: Thailand (Bangkok), Brazil (Brasilia), Hungary (Budapest), Germany (Berlin)

M: Philippines (Manila), Spain (Madrid), Russia (Moscow), Oman (Muscat)

S: South Korea (Seoul), Bulgaria (Sofia), Sweden (Stockholm), Bosnia and Herzegovina (Sarajevo)

(12) TABLE FOR ONE

All of the items on the menu describe dishes named after well-known individuals. In order, the dishes are:

▶ Bellini (named after painter Giovanni Bellini)
▶ Oysters Rockefeller (named after industrialist John D. Rockefeller)
▶ Beef Stroganoff (named after Russian diplomat Count Pavel Stroganov)
▶ Pavlova (named after dancer Anna Pavlova)
▶ Peach Melba (named after opera singer Nellie Melba)

(13) UNDERCOVER

B Y T by J M – Big Yellow Taxi by Joni Mitchell.

All of the entries are the initials of songs and the artists who performed them, but "Big Yellow Taxi" is the only entry that is an original song by the performer listed. All of the other entries are cover versions of songs, originally performed by a different artist:

▶ "Hallelujah" by Jeff Buckley (originally by Leonard Cohen)
▶ "Hurt" by Johnny Cash (originally by Nine Inch Nails)

▶ "All Along the Watchtower" by Jimi Hendrix Experience (originally by Bob Dylan)

▶ "I'm A Believer" by Smash Mouth (originally by Neil Diamond, recorded by The Monkees)

▶ "Respect" by Aretha Franklin (originally by Otis Redding)

▶ "I Will Always Love You" by Whitney Houston (originally by Dolly Parton)

(14) POETRY CORNER

The property is Westminster Abbey – the "names" mentioned in the list are all buried there. The title also clues "Poet's Corner," the name given to the area in which all of these memorials are found.

(15) CORRESPONDENCE

The most appropriate solution is 3: Envelope.

Each pair of words in the puzzle conceals a third word which, when added to the end of the first word, and to the beginning of the second, can create two further words. In the first pair (SOME and NOT), the word WHAT is concealed, giving SOMEWHAT and WHATNOT. The full set of concealed words is as follows, in the order given in the puzzle:

WHAT: giving SOMEWHAT and WHATNOT

CAN: giving OVERSCAN and CANVASES

BEST: giving DRABBEST and BESTOWED

FIT: giving OUTFIT and FITTEST

THROUGH: giving BREAKTHROUGH and THROUGHFLOW

POST: giving SIGNPOST and POSTCARD

BOX: giving CHATTERBOX and BOXBOARD

When read in order, the concealed words create the question "WHAT CAN BEST FIT THROUGH POST BOX?" The most appropriate answer to this from the given options is "envelope."

(16) HEBDOMADAL PROBLEM

Each of the song lyrics is taken from a song with a day of the week in its title. They can then be arranged into pairs according to which day of the week they reference:

Tuesday

▶ "Ruby Tuesday" by The Rolling Stones (She would never say where she came from, etc.)

▶ "Tuesday's Gone" by Lynyrd Skynyrd (Train roll on, on down the line etc.)

Friday

▶ "Friday" by Rebecca Black (7 AM, waking up in the morning, etc.)

▶ "Last Friday Night (T.G.I.F)" by Katy Perry (There's a stranger in my bed, etc.)

Saturday

▶ "Saturday Night's Alright (For Fighting)" by Elton John (It's getting late have you seen my mates, etc.)

▶ "Someday I'll Be Saturday Night" by Bon Jovi (Hey, man I'm alive, etc.)

Sunday

▶ "Sunday Girl" by Blondie (I know a girl from a lonely street, etc.)

▶ "Everyday is Like Sunday" by Morrissey (Trudging slowly over wet sand, etc.)

(17) ALPHABET SUMS

a) $U = 0$ $N = 1$ $E = 2$ $A = 3$ $L = 4$ $T = 5$ $I = 6$ $G = 7$ $M = 8$ $R = 9$

   i.e. $3431 + 509617 = 729831 - 216783$

b) $R = 0$ $N = 1$ $G = 2$ $U = 3$ $A = 4$ $T = 5$ $I = 6$ $L = 7$ $E = 8$ $M = 9$

   i.e. $4741 + 530612 = 816294 - 280941$

(18) NOT TO BE?

All of the films and musicals described are said to be based on Shakespeare plays, as follows:

- ▶ *West Side Story* (*Romeo and Juliet*)
- ▶ *She's the Man* (*Twelfth Night*)
- ▶ *10 Things I Hate About You* (*The Taming of the Shrew*)
- ▶ *The Lion King* (*Hamlet*)
- ▶ *Ran* (*King Lear*)
- ▶ *Kiss Me Kate* (*The Taming of the Shrew*)

(19) GNEISS TRY

The clues can be solved as follows:

List A	List B
collier rope = miner cord	data unit = kilobyte
deadly gnash = killer bite	hebdomadal lodger = weekly boarder
feebly boundary = weakly border	maritime party = naval ball
humbugs encounter = mints meet	ocean atmosphere = sea air
spot inheritor = see heir	pulverize flesh = mince meat
umbilicus cry = navel bawl	sad notes = minor chord

Each item in List A can be paired with a homophonic item in List B. For example, "killer bite" and "kilobyte" are homophones of one another.

The full list of pairs is as follows:
miner cord / minor chord
killer bite / kilobyte
weakly border / weekly boarder
mints meet / mincemeat
see heir / sea air
navel bawl / naval ball

Homophones are clued in the title, where "gneiss" is a homophone of "nice," and in the question "according to what's 'here'," where "here" is a homophone of "hear."

⑳ CLIMBING

The etymologies of these words are all numerical, so the correct ascending order would be as follows, with the number which each word etymologically derives from listed in brackets:

- ▶ Unity (one)
- ▶ Triassic (three)
- ▶ Decimate (ten)
- ▶ Fortnight (fourteen)
- ▶ Score (twenty)
- ▶ Quarantine (forty)

㉑ CHEMYSTERY

It's not harmful.

Expanding out the notation "$_2$" to produce double letters gives the letter string CINNOOSUU. These letters can be rearranged, or "restructured," to generate the word "INNOCUOUS," suggesting that the resulting chemical is harmless.

(22) 'TIS THE SEASON

A gold ring. All of the words in column A can be preceded by the word "gold" to form a new item, and all of the words in column B can similarly be followed by the word "ring":

Gold card	Smoke ring
Gold dust	Key ring
Gold plate	Tree ring
Gold thread	Fairy ring
Gold rush	Onion ring

There are five words in each column, creating five gold rings – just as there are five gold rings in *The Twelve Days of Christmas*.

(23) DREAM BIG

The hiding person is Martin Luther King, whose name can be made out of the matching last names of the three pairs:

▶ Dean Martin (comic partner of Jerry Lewis)
▶ Chris Martin (lead singer of Coldplay)
▶ Martin Luther (leading figure of the Reformation)
▶ John Luther (the eponymous character of the BBC TV series starring Idris Elba)
▶ Stephen King (author of *The Shining*)
▶ Carole King (American singer who released *Tapestry* in 1971)

(24) LAST WORD

A different word can be added to each set in turn. Together the words spell out SOME LIKE IT HOT, a 1959 film starring Marilyn Monroe.

- ▶ SOME: awesome, tiresome, twosome, wholesome
- ▶ LIKE: alike, godlike, ladylike, childlike
- ▶ IT: cubit, pulpit, permit, orbit
- ▶ HOT: earshot, snapshot, upshot, potshot

(25) GET THERE EVENTUALLY

The clues describe the following phrases:

- ▶ Blow by blow
- ▶ Step by step
- ▶ Side by side
- ▶ Little by little
- ▶ Two by two

"By" is the short particle that the solutions have in common. The conjunction "and" can be added in an inverted but similar fashion to the previous solutions to create the phrase "by and by." By further way of confirmation, "by and by" also means "eventually," as hinted at in the title.

(26) KEY PATH

The keys used to type each word are adjacent to one another on a standard computer keyboard, tracing the word on the keyboard in the order that the letters in each word are typed.

(27) PLENTY OF MOVEMENT

The solved clues all contain words that describe the movement of water. In order, the solutions to the clues are:

- <u>Drip</u>-feed
- <u>Flow</u> chart
- Live <u>stream</u>
- Meteor <u>shower</u>
- <u>Flood</u>light
- <u>Trickle</u>-down
- <u>Spray</u> tan

(28) CAUGHT OUT

They all describe homophones or homographs of pieces of equipment used in sports. Where the solution to the clue is a homophone, it is listed in brackets:

- Tee (tea)
- Puck
- Bat
- Ball (bawl)
- Club
- Cue

(29) A DEARTH OF EVADERS

Drop a fifth, "E" (the fifth letter) from "A Dearth of Evaders" to clue "[a] Darth [of] Vaders," which in turn clues Darth Vader, or "VADER," the antagonist of the original *Star Wars* films.

The numbers 1, 2, 3, 4, and 5 correspond in turn to the letters V, A, D, E, and R. Substituting them into the grid accordingly gives the following:

The remaining letter in the grid – corresponding to the number 6 – could be either "I," as shown, or could alternatively also be "O," giving "odea" (an alternative plural of "odeum").

The character is therefore hiding in the shaded squares, which can be anagrammed to make his name.

(30) NATURAL WORLD

The solutions to these clues all contain part of a plant. In order, the clues reveal:

- Ta<u>stem</u>aker
- <u>Bud</u>dha
- Che<u>root</u>
- Stal<u>k</u>er
- <u>Leaf</u>let

(31) PRIME EXCEPTION

Each letter of the alphabet has been assigned a number in ascending order, where A = 1, B = 2, C = 3, and so on through until Z = 26. Then the numbers which make up each word have been added together, with the exception of prime numbers, as per the title: "prime exception." The totals of each word are as follows, with prime numbers crossed out and not included in the total:

- BILE: 2̶ + 9 + 12 + 5̶ = 21
- FRANCE: 6 + 18 + 1 + 14 + 3̶ + 5̶ = 39
- QUENCHED: 1̶7̶ + 21 + 5̶ + 14 + 3̶ + 8 + 5̶ + 4 = 47
- WEBS = 2̶3̶ + 5̶ + 2̶ + 1̶9̶ = 0
- AWAKE = 1 + 2̶3̶ + 1 + 1̶1̶ + 5̶ = 2
- GEMS = 7̶ + 5̶ + 1̶3̶ + 1̶9̶ = 0

Following this rule, COFFEE = 3 + 15 + 6 + 6 + 5̶ + 5̶ = 27

㉜ NO ROOM FOR A TOXIC MIMIC

The words are all spelled with letters which have horizontal or vertical symmetry, or both, when written in upper case.

Letters with vertical symmetry are A, H, I, M, O, T, U, W, V, and X, creating the following group:

AUTOMATA	OX
HOAX	VOMIT
MAMMOTH	WITHOUT
MAXIMUM	

Letters with horizontal symmetry, are B, C, D, E, I, K, O, and X, creating the following group:

BEDECKED	DIOXIDE
BOXED	EXCEEDED
CODEBOOK	OX
DICED	

The letters O and X have both vertical and horizontal symmetry, so the word "OX" appears in both lists. (The letter I also has both vertical and horizontal symmetry, as an aside).

The two words "MIMIC" and "TOXIC" – as shown in the title – also contain only letters with either vertical and horizontal symmetry, but as they both contain a mixture of the two, they could not be applied to either list, so there is "no room" for them.

(33) METHOD IN THE METHOD

An "estimate."

First, each clue can be solved as follows:

BALMIEST + ?	➔	ESTIMABLE
TABLE + ?	➔	STABLE
ABLE + ?	➔	TABLE
STABLE + ?	➔	BESTIAL
BESTIAL + ?	➔	BALMIEST
LB + ?	➔	LAB
ESTIMABLE + ?	➔	TIMETABLES
LAB + ?	➔	ABLE

Each transformed word uses the letters from the original word, plus one extra letter. These extra letters are represented by the "?" symbols.

In turn, the extra letters needed are E, S, T, I, M, A, T, and E, spelling "estimate."

The additional feature is that all of the resulting words on the right-hand side form a word pyramid, providing a natural ordering from shortest to longest (or vice-versa).

(34) BORN IN THE USA

They all include the letter sequence "USA" within their names – and they are also all US towns.

(35) LAY THE TABLE

Each word in the list contains the symbol for a chemical element. The elements appear in order of atomic number, increasing from 1 to 5 reading down the list. The symbol for each element – made of one or two letters – has been shifted to the right in its word by the same number of places as its atomic number. So, for example, the answer to "SAHRE" is "SHARE" because the "H" has been moved 1 place to the right.

The unshifted words and elements are as follows:

▶ SHARE: Hydrogen (H = 1)
▶ SCHEDULED: Helium (He = 2)
▶ ABOLISHERS: Lithium (Li = 3)
▶ EMBELLISHER: Beryllium (Be = 4)
▶ OBLIGATE: Boron (B = 5)

(36) CORRESPONDENCE

The most appropriate solution is 3: Envelope.

Each pair of words in the puzzle conceals a third word which, when added to the end of the first word, and to the beginning of the second, can create two further words. In the first pair (SOME and NOT), the word WHAT is concealed, giving SOMEWHAT and WHATNOT.

The full set of concealed words is as follows, in the order given in the puzzle:

WHAT: giving SOMEWHAT and WHATNOT

CAN: giving OVERSCAN and CANVASES

BEST: giving DRABBEST and BESTOWED

FIT: giving OUTFIT and FITTEST

THROUGH: giving BREAKTHROUGH and THROUGHFLOW

POST: giving SIGNPOST and POSTCARD

BOX: giving CHATTERBOX and BOXBOARD

When read in order, the concealed words create the question "WHAT CAN BEST FIT THROUGH POST BOX?" The most appropriate answer to this from the given options is "envelope."

(37) INTELLECTUAL PROPERTY

They are all descriptions of names of colleges at the Universities of Oxford and Cambridge which share the same name:

▶ Corpus Christi
▶ Pembroke
▶ Jesus
▶ Wolfson
▶ St Catharine's (now spelled "St Catherine's" in Oxford, although it originally had the same spelling)
▶ Trinity

(38) WHAT DID YOU SAY?

The puzzle title is an instruction here, since saying the solutions to the clues aloud may reveal that they are all homophones of parts of the body:

▶ Mussels (muscles)   ▶ Vane (vein)

▶ Alms (arms)   ▶ Hare (hair)

▶ Scull (skull)   ▶ Waste (waist)

(39) BUILD YOUR OWN PALINDROME 2

The answers in alphabetical order are: ACETATE, BALLET, BELLIES, CANADA, ESTELLA, LESION, MARSEILLE, NOISELESS, OPENER, POSSE, RAMADAN, SERENE.

The palindrome they form is: NOISELESS, OPENER, ESTELLA, BELLIES, RAMADAN, ACETATE, CANADA, MARSEILLE, BALLET, SERENE, POSSE, LESION.

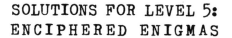

① STANDBY

Words in a position to work are: dethre, gdola, iric, madna, miker, and tal

All of the letter strings can be restored to full words either by adding "on" or "off" to the middle of each word, as follows:

cOFFee   prOFFered
dethrONe   reOFFends
gONdola   scOFFed
irONic   tONal
madONna   tOFFee
mONiker   unOFFicial

Any words restored with the word "ON" can be considered to be "in a position to work."

The ON/OFF connection is clued in the title, with "standby" being a state of being both partially on and partially off.

2 THE AZ OF THE US

The final equation takes you to Maine.

The question "What must be voided"? requires two different interpretations to solve the equations.

In the first interpretation, some letters in the name of each US state must be "voided" to leave behind the two-letter abbreviations. For example, the letters A, A, W, and I must be voided to transform "Hawaii" into "HI." State abbreviations are clued in the title, as AZ is the abbreviation for Arizona.

The full list of abbreviations used are as follows:

Alabama = AL   Iowa = IA

Delaware = DE   Minnesota = MN

Hawaii = HI   Pennsylvania = PA

For the second interpretation of "What must be voided", the letters of the word VOIDED should be substituted, in this case with numbers corresponding to their positions in the alphabet:

V = 22

O = 15

I = 9

D = 4

E = 5

D = 4

When these two interpretations are combined, the first equation reads:

HI + 22 = DE

"+ 22" indicates that the letters on the left must be shifted forwards through the alphabet by that amount to give the result, i.e. using a Caesar shift. In this case, the letters "HI" shifted forwards by 22 results in "DE," or Delaware.

The full list of resulting equations is as follows:

HI	+22	=	DE
AL	+15	=	PA
DE	+9	=	MN
DE	+4	=	HI
HI	+5	=	MN
IA	+4	=	?

In the final row, the letters IA must be shifted forwards by four letters to give "ME," or Maine. The answer to the second question, "Where does the final eq

③ SMILE AND WAVE

Column B consists of words that would be visible if the corresponding word from column A were semaphored but viewed from behind. The corresponding pairs are as follows:

CIGS	EXAM
EGO	CAW
BCC	FEE
MOGS	SWAM
NUNS	UNUM
MENS	SCUM
AXUM	GINS

(4) SQUARE ROUTES®

(5) ODIOUS CONNECTION

John Keats. When read aloud, the solutions to the clues form the subjects of famous odes written by Keats:

- ► "A Grecian Urn": agree (concur), shun (avoid), earn (gain money) – *Ode on a Grecian Urn*
- ► "Indolence": inn (hotel), doll (child's human-like toy), ents (tree-like beings in *Lord of the Rings*) – *Ode on Indolence*
- ► "Melancholy": melon (sweet fruit), collie (sheepdog) – *Ode on Melancholy*
- ► "A Nightingale": a (first letter), knight (heroic champion), tin (metal container), gale (strong wind) – *Ode to a Nightingale*
- ► "Psyche": sigh (expressive exhalation), key (lock-operating device) – *Ode to Psyche*

⑥ ODD ONE OUT

FACTUAL.

The property common to each word is that one letter can be "deducted" to form another word of the same or similar meaning. Words can be paired according to the letters that they lose, so AMI(C)ABLE and (C)RUDE form a pair because they both lose their C. The other pairs are AC(R)ID and BU(R)ST; (B)RASH and SUPER(B); CLEAN(S)ER and (S)ELECT; and EGO(T)IST and RO(T) UND. The odd one out is (F)ACTUAL, which is the only word that loses an F.

⑦ ANCIENT EQUATIONS

5, 4, 10, and 500.

In each equation, the second number given should be written out in words, giving "seven," "five," "sixty," and "hundred."

The first number in each equation then refers to the number of letters which should be removed from each side of the word to leave some letters remaining in the middle:

a   Taking two letters from either side of seven leaves "v"

b   Taking one letter from either side of five leaves "iv"

c   Taking two letters from either side of sixty leaves "x"

d   Taking three letters from either side of hundred leaves "d"

The remaining letters "v," "iv," "x," and "d" are all Roman numerals, which give the solution for each equation when "translated" back into Arabic numerals.

The solutions are therefore:

a. 5   b. 4   c. 10   d. 500

(8) A SILVER SPOON

The solution to the second clue in each bullet point is a "spoonerism," where the first letter of two words have been switched to create a new expression:

Bad manners → mad banners

Makes time → takes mime

Sweet tooth → tweet sooth

Back seat → sack beat

(9) COVER VERSIONS

1j, 2b, 3d, 4k, 5a, 6h, 7e, 8i, 9f+c, 10g

The first sentence of the question is deliberately misleading in that it *isn't* the songs, but rather their original artists' names, that have been literally "covered" by – i.e. enclosed within – the names of the different groups. For example, "Believe" was originally performed by CHER, whose name appears in THE SEAR<u>CHER</u>S – hence "Believe" is matched with THE SEARCHERS.

Likewise "Girl From Mars" was by ASH, who appear in KUL<u>A SH</u>AKER; "How Long" was by ACE, who appear in R<u>ACE</u>Y; "Losing My Religion" was by R.E.M, who appear in THE SUP<u>REM</u>ES; "Mamma Mia" was by ABBA, who appear in BLACK S<u>ABBA</u>TH; "Mr Blue Sky" was by E.L.O, who appear in THE B<u>ELO</u>VED; "Rock 'N' Roll Children" was by DIO, who appear in RA<u>DIO</u>HEAD; "Smooth Operator" was by SADE, who appear in THE PA<u>SADE</u>NAS; and "These Dreams" was by HEART, who appear in THE <u>ART</u> OF NOISE. "Someone Like You" was performed by ADELE, whose name has been covered by the remaining two groups, SL<u>ADE</u> and L<u>E</u>VEL 42.

(10) A NOVEL APPROACH

A P O T A A A Y M by J J: *A Portrait of the Artist as a Young Man* by James Joyce. This is the only work of literature listed which was originally published in English. All of the others can be sorted into pairs by the language they were originally published in. The works are listed in order below, with the original language of publication in brackets:

Don Quixote by Miguel de Cervantes (Spanish)
Les Misérables by Victor Hugo (French)
Love in the Time of Cholera by Gabriel García Márquez (Spanish)
War and Peace by Leo Tolstoy (Russian)
Madame Bovary by Gustave Flaubert (French)
Crime and Punishment by Fyodor Dostoevsky (Russian)

(11) ANOTHER GIRL

Charlotte, since this is the only name in the list which does not feature in the title of a song by The Beatles. "Another Girl" is also a Beatles' song title. The complete song names are as follows:

- ▶ "Eleanor Rigby"
- ▶ "Julia"
- ▶ "Long Tall Sally"
- ▶ "Lovely Rita"
- ▶ "Dear Prudence"
- ▶ "Martha My Dear"
- ▶ "Sexy Sadie"

(12) RESTORES THE BALANCE

The words clued by list C are:

Pertaining to annals = calendrical

Allure = enticement

Consuming = ingesting

Method of Braille printing = interpoint

Fits together neatly = tessellates

Provide insufficient finances = underfund

Each of the solution words in List C can be made by linking together an anagrammed item from List A, an anagrammed item from list B, and then that same anagrammed item from List A again – so list A is applied twice.

For example, "calendrical" can be made by taking "LAC" from List A and "DINER" from List B and by using the letters from each item to create a new anagram, such as CAL + ENDRI + CAL = "calendrical."

The remaining items can be matched up as follows, to create the given strings:

List A	List B	List C			
LAC	DINER	calendrical	LAC+DINER+LAC	→	CAL+ENDRI+CAL
TEN	MICE	enticement	TEN+MICE+TEN	→	ENT+ICEM+ENT
GIN	SET	ingesting	GIN+SET+GIN	→	ING+EST+ING
TIN	PORE	interpoint	TIN+PORE+TIN	→	INT+ERPO+INT
SET	SALLE	tessellates	SET+SALLE+SET	→	TES+SELLA+TES
DUN	REF	underfund	DUN+REF+DUN	→	UND+ERF+UND

The word "restores" in the title is an example of a word which begins and ends with the same three letters, and the "balance" in the title clues the need to "balance" the identical letters at the beginning and end of each solution word.

(13) VERY THOUGHTFUL

When read aloud, the clues describe philosophers:

- ▶ Kierkegaard (kirk, egg, guard)
- ▶ Socrates (sock, rat, ease)
- ▶ Descartes (day, cart)
- ▶ Aristotle (A, wrist, tot, all)
- ▶ Plato (play, toe)

(14) MULTITASKER

The words on the left are anagrams of the last names of well-known people, the words on the right being anagrams of their various professions. For example, BALCONETS is an anagram of [John] CONSTABLE, a famous ARTIST, which in turn is an anagram of STRAIT – hence BALCONETS is paired with STRAIT.

Likewise BRANDRETH ([Sarah] BERNHARDT) is paired with CASTERS (ACTRESS); GRISTLE ([George] STIGLER) is paired with EMOTICONS (ECONOMIST); LIGATURE ([Jean Paul] GAULTIER) is paired with RESIGNED (DESIGNER); MORALLY ([George] MALLORY) is paired with ENUMERATION (MOUNTAINEER); PHRASED ([Alan] SHEPARD) is paired with UNNATURAL (LUNARNAUT); TARNATION ([Quentin] TARANTINO) is paired with CREDITOR (DIRECTOR); TENPINS ([Sir Matthew] PINSENT) is paired with PALIMONY (OLYMPIAN); and TRILOBE ([Louis] BLERIOT) is paired with MARINA (AIRMAN).

The exceptional word is TARDINESS, which is an anagram of [Barbra] STREISAND – a truly exceptional multitasker, being a multi-award winning ACTRESS, DIRECTOR, *and* SINGER.

⒂ CONTROL PANEL

The letters in the puzzle indicate the letters used in computer control key functions ("Ctrl" on a PC, "Cmd" on a Mac): Ctrl + X = cut, Ctrl + V = paste, Ctrl + P = print, Ctrl + C = copy, and Ctrl + Y (often) = redo.

Each letter in the puzzle should be replaced with the word of the function it represents, and the words in the instructions arranged in the gaps in the order "HAIR," "BOARD," "BLUE," "PHOTO," "LENT," reading from top to bottom. The "+" symbol indicates that the two words in each equation should be combined to create a single new word. These new words are therefore as follows:

HAIR + X = HAIRCUT

V + BOARD = PASTEBOARD

BLUE + P = BLUEPRINT

PHOTO + C = PHOTOCOPY

Y + LENT = REDOLENT

⒃ MONORAIL OFFENCE

Three. All of the station names have been encrypted using a rail fence cipher, with three rails used to encrypt each name.

Letters in each station name have been encoded by writing them in a zigzag line up and down the three "rails," as shown below, starting from the top left and working left to right. The letters are then read off from each row in turn to give the coded sequence.

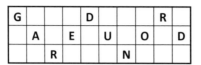

G			D			R	
	A	E	U		O		D
		R			N		

Or "GARE DU NORD"

A			E			N			T			L
	N	W		R	E		C	N	R		A	
		T			P			E			A	

Or "ANTWERPEN CENTRAAL"

L			R			L			E	
	I	E		P	O		S	R	E	
		V			O			T		T

Or "LIVERPOOL STREET"

G			D			T		
	R	N		C	N		R	L
		A			E			A

Or "GRAND CENTRAL"

P			S			I	
	E	N		T	T	O	
		N			A		N

Or "PENN STATION"

P				I				O	
	A		D		N		T		N
		D				G			

Or "PADDINGTON"

(17) CULTURAL OMISSIONS

The entries can be organized into musicals, operas and novels. Each entry in the list has had the letters of either "MUSICAL," "OPERA," or "NOVEL" removed, depending on which category it belongs in. All spaces have been kept in the correct place. The restored titles are as follows, ordered into the correct categories:

Musicals:
▶ CAROUSEL (ROE)
▶ HAIRSPRAY (HRPRY)
▶ COMPANY (OPNY)
▶ CHICAGO (HGO)

Operas:
▶ CARMEN (CMN)
▶ TOSCA (TSC)
▶ DIDO AND AENEAS (DID ND NS)
▶ PAGLIACCI (GLICCI)

Novels:
▶ JANE EYRE (JA YR)
▶ GULLIVER'S TRAVELS (GUIR'S TRAS)
▶ LITTLE WOMEN (ITT WM)
▶ EMMA (MMA)

(18) FIGURE IT OUT

These abbreviations are all novels that include numbers written as words in their titles. Taken in turn they are:

▶ *Around the World in Eighty Days* by Jules Verne
▶ *One Flew Over the Cuckoo's Nest* by Ken Kesey
▶ *One Hundred Years of Solitude* by Gabriel García Márquez
▶ *Slaughterhouse-Five* by Kurt Vonnegut

(19) FUSION CORE

The missing countries, in order of the first list as originally ordered, are Laos, Spain, Nauru, Guatemala, and Nepal. To reveal these, the names of chemical elements should be replaced with their chemical symbols:

Oxygen = O   Tellurium = Te

Phosphorous = P   Uranium = U

Protactinium = Pa

Once these substitutions have been made, an element from List 2 can be inserted between a country from List 1 and a country from List 3, revealing a third hidden country name. For example, O (oxygen) can be inserted between Angola and Samoa to create "AngolaOSamoa," revealing "Laos" in the middle.

The six hidden countries can therefore be revealed as follows:

Angola+O+Samoa = AngolaOSamoa = Laos

Cyprus+Pa+India = CyprusPaIndia = Spain

Guyana+U+Russia = GuyanaURussia = Nauru

Nicaragua+Te+Malawi = NicaraguaTeMalawi = Guatemala

Ukraine+P+Algeria = UkrainePAlgeria = Nepal

This means in turn that the correct list rearrangements are as follows:

List 1	List 2	List 3
Angola	Oxygen	Samoa
Cyprus	Protactinium	India
Guyana	Uranium	Russia
Nicaragua	Tellurium	Malawi
Ukraine	Phosphorous	Algeria

▶ *Twenty Thousand Leagues Under the Sea* by Jules Verne

⑳ CONNOISSEUR OPERATION

The theme is European countries, with the four new groups linked by one of the countries Austria, Italy, Sweden, and the United Kingdom. "Europe" is also clued in the title: "Connoiss<u>eur</u> <u>Ope</u>ration."

List A contains airport codes for airports that can be found in major cities in each country, which are also words in their own right:

  GOT (Gothenburg, Sweden)   NAP (Naples, Italy)

  MAN (Manchester, UK)   VIE (Vienna, Austria)

List B contains the names of official languages used in each country, with letters rearranged into alphabetical order:

  aaiilnt – Italian (Italy)   dehissw – Swedish (Sweden)

  aegmnr – German (Austria)   eghilns – English (UK)

List C contains the names of currencies used by each country before the introduction of the Euro (in the cases of Italy and Austria), where any letters of the word "currency" have been deleted:

Koa – Krona (Sweden)

Pod stlig – Pound sterling (UK)

Lia – Lira (Italy)

Shillig – Schilling (Austria)

List D contains the names of units of measurement that are named after scientists, each of whose nationalities correspond to a given country:

Celsius (after Anders Celsius, Swedish)

Newton (after Isaac Newton, English)

Mach (after Ernst Mach, Austrian)

Volt (after Alessandro Volta, Italian)

The words should therefore be grouped as follows:

Austria:
VIE, aegmnr, Shillig, Mach

Sweden:
GOT, dehissw, Koa, Celsius

Italy:
NAP, aaiilnt, Lia, Volt

UK:
MAN, eghilns, Pod stlig, Newton

㉑ DOPPELGÄNGERS

The words have been encoded using a letter-to-number substitution where A = 1, B = 2, and so on. In cases where double letters ("doppelgängers") appear, however, the corresponding numbers have been doubled rather than repeated. This means that AA = 1 + 1 = 2, BB = 2 + 2 = 4, etc, so for example "HAAR" would be coded as "8 2 18," where the 2 represents a double A.

The original words are:

ADDRESSEE	JELLY
BALLOON	KEENNESS
BOOKKEEPER	PILLOW
COMMITTEE	SILLY
GRILL	SUCCESS
HAPPINESS	ZOOKEEPER

These words can be split into three groups of four, based on the number of double letters per word. The appropriate groupings of the original codes are therefore:

One set of double letters:

7 18 9 24 (GRILL)
10 5 24 25 (JELLY)
16 9 24 15 23 (PILLOW)
19 9 24 25 (SILLY)

Two sets of double letters:

2 1 24 30 14 (BALLOON)
8 1 32 9 14 5 38 (HAPPINESS)
19 21 6 5 38 (SUCCESS)
26 30 11 10 16 5 18 (ZOOKEEPER)

Three sets of double letters:

1 8 18 5 38 10 (ADDRESSEE)
2 30 22 10 16 5 18 (BOOKKEEPER)
3 15 26 9 40 10 (COMMITTEE)

(22) CREATURE COMFORTS

The titles of the abbreviated songs all include animals:

- ▶ <u>Hounds</u> of Love by Kate Bush
- ▶ <u>Anaconda</u> by Nicki Minaj
- ▶ Eye of the <u>Tiger</u> by Survivor
- ▶ Karma <u>Chameleon</u> by Culture Club
- ▶ Wild <u>Horses</u> by The Rolling Stones

The first letters of each animal, in order, spell the word "HATCH." The chameleon is the only animal in this list that lays eggs, and therefore is the only animal applicable to "hatch."

Note that while most snakes do also lay eggs, anacondas (like all boas) do not lay eggs, although their young do develop internally in egg-like sacs.

(23) STREPTOCOCCAL INFECTION

I T M H by W P, i.e. "In the Midnight Hour" by Wilson Pickett. It is the only song which doesn't include a shade of red in the title. In order, the songs are:

- ▶ "Bad Blood" by Taylor Swift
- ▶ "Ruby" by Kaiser Chiefs
- ▶ "The Court of the Crimson King" by King Crimson
- ▶ "In the Midnight Hour" by Wilson Pickett
- ▶ "Strawberry Fields Forever" by The Beatles
- ▶ "Brick House" by Commodores
- ▶ "Black Horse and the Cherry Tree" by KT Tunstall

(24) FAMILIAR CONNECTIONS

They were all given exactly the same name as their father, excluding suffixes. In order, the clues describe:

▶ Kurt Vonnegut
▶ Al Gore
▶ Marlon Brando
▶ Robert Downey Jr
▶ Henry VIII
▶ Donald Trump Jr
▶

(25) VALUABLE FLOWERS

18. A suitable corresponding flower is a honeysuckle, as given in the question, although there are other possibilities such as forget-me-not and globeflower.

Vowels and consonants have been given different numerical values to reach each solution in these equations. Each vowel = 1 and each consonant = 2 in every word, and the resulting values have been added together. Any mathematical operations have then been applied to give the total for each word.

In the final equation, GARDENIA = 12 and IRIS = 6, making a total of 18. HONEYSUCKLE is a flower with a total value of 18 following this system.

(26) CONTINENTAL DISCOVERIES

Set 5 (RBFV...). Each line contains most of the letters of the alphabet, but some are missing. Those missing letters can be anagrammed to reveal the following capital cities:

1.	PARIS	20.	MOGADISHU
2.	ZAGREB	21.	BUDAPEST
3.	LISBON	22.	PRAGUE
4.	EDINBURGH	23.	BERLIN

Mogadishu is the only non-European capital city on the list, making it the odd one out.

(27) RIGGED

They all describe fictional ships. In order, they are:

▸ Black Pig (*Captain Pugwash*)
▸ African Queen (*The African Queen*)
▸ Flying Dutchman (legend)
▸ Dawn Treader (*The Chronicles of Narnia*)
▸ Jeroboam (*Moby Dick*)

(28) VEXILLOLOGICAL VEXATION

The key "SEMAPHORE" (but not semaphore code itself) can be used to decode the flags, and therefore CJFFY NJOPN is the odd one out.

The popular names of seven flags have been encoded with a keyword cipher, using the key "SEMAPHORE," as hinted at by the reference to "flags" in the prompt. This creates the cipher string SEMAPHORBCDFGIJKLNQTUVWXYZ, so the encoding changed

A to S, and B to E, and C to M, and so on. The decoded list of flags therefore reads as follows:

UNION JACK

JOLLY ROGER

SALTIRE

STARS AND STRIPES

TRICOLORE

BROKEN TRIDENT

GOLDEN ARROWHEAD

All of the flags in the list are the informal names of national flags, except for the Jolly Roger, which is a symbol of piracy. Jolly Roger, therefore, is the odd one out – which is CJFFY NJOPN.

Authors

The following puzzle authors created all of the puzzles for this book:

ELIZABETH CROWDY

Elizabeth Crowdy is a puzzle researcher and editor who has worked on a wide range of titles. She is also a poet and keen creative writer in other fields, and has worked on original scripts, poetry and music with Acorn Music Theatre Company. She holds a degree in English from the University of Cambridge.

RICHARD HEALD

Richard Heald is a mathematics graduate and IT worker who lives in South Yorkshire, England. He has been a long-time fan, and occasional setter, of puzzles and quizzes, and was a series semi-finalist on the UK TV quiz shows Only Connect and Countdown. He has a particular love of competitive crossword solving and has on several occasions been the annual champion of The Observer newspaper's Azed clue-writing competition (see www. andlit.org.uk). With Ian Simpson he produces a Square Routes® puzzle for The Times newspaper every Saturday.

LAURA JAYNE AYRES

Laura Jayne Ayres is a professional puzzle writer and editor, with a degree in Linguistics from the University of Cambridge. She is also a published playwright.

GARETH MOORE

Gareth Moore is the best-selling author of over 200 books of puzzles for both children and adults, with total worldwide sales in excess of 5 million copies. His work has been published in more than 35 different languages, and his puzzles can also be found in newspapers, magazines, apps and websites. He is a director of the UK Puzzle Association, and a former board member of the World Puzzle Federation.

IAN SIMPSON

Ian Simpson is an engineer who lives in Edinburgh, Scotland. He is a fan of mathematical and word puzzles, and has set several Listener crosswords under the pseudonym Homer. He is the co-inventor (with Richard Heald) of the Square Routes® puzzle, which appears each Saturday in the UK newspaper The Times.